zermatt
matterhorn

first edition 2004

written and edited by
Isobel Rostron & Michael Kayson

Qanuk Publishing & Design Ltd
www.snowmole.com

the snowmole guide to **zermatt matterhorn**
first edition 2004

published by Qanuk Publishing & Design Ltd
45 Mysore Road London SW11 5RY

copyright © Qanuk Publishing & Design Ltd 2004
maps © Qanuk Publishing & Design Ltd 2004
artwork © oliver brodrick-ward 2003

printed by Craftprint, Singapore

ISBN 0-9545739-6-X

A catalogue record of this book is available from the British Library.

All rights reserved. No part of this publication may be reproduced, stored in a retrieval system, or transmitted at any time or by any means electronic, mechanical, photocopying, recording or otherwise, without the prior written permission of the publisher.

snowmole does not accept any advertising or payment, and the guides are written free from any bias.

The contents of this book are believed correct at the time of printing. As things can change, errors or omissions may occur. The publishers and authors can accept no responsibility for any loss, injury or inconvenience sustained by anybody using information or comment contained in this guide.

contents

4	how to use the guide
5	how to use the maps
6	explanation of icons

text
introducing zermatt
10	overview
13	seasonal variations
14	quintessential zermatt

getting started
18	planning your trip
20	getting there
25	getting around
28	accommodation
42	lift passes
44	skis, boots & boards
46	lessons & guiding

the skiing
54	overview
58	rothorn
63	gornergrat
67	klein matterhorn
73	breuil-cervinia
78	suggested days
80	off-piste
82	ski touring
84	events & activities

the resort
88	eating out
98	après-ski & nightlife
106	activities
108	children
110	seasonnaires

the a-z
114	tour operators
115	directory
122	glossary
124	index

maps
route & resort maps
fc	zermatt
21	self-drive
23	fly-drive
27	bus
31	hotels
89	eating out
99	après-ski & nightlife

ski maps
individual areas & ski area overview ➜ back cover flap

how to use the guide

How much you enjoy your winter holiday depends on a variety of things. Some you cannot influence - you can't guarantee sunshine, good snow, or your flight landing on time... but most things should be within your control. With the majority of ski holidays lasting just a week or less, you don't want to waste time trying to find a good restaurant, or struggling with an overgrown piste map. The snowmole guides are designed with 2 purposes in mind: to save you time by providing essential information on the operation of the resort, and to help you to make the most of your time by giving insight into every aspect of your stay.

The guide is not intended to be read from cover to cover. After the introduction to the resort, the guide is split into 4 distinct sections - getting started, the skiing, the resort and the a-z - so you can dip into the information you need when you need it. Some information will be useful to you beforehand, some while you are in resort and some while you are on the mountain.

getting started deals with the basics: how to get to the resort, how to get around once you're there, and your options when buying your lift pass, renting equipment and booking lessons or mountain guides.

the skiing gives an overview of the mountains and the ski area, information on the off-piste, and a breakdown for beginners, intermediates, experts, boarders and non-skiers. The ski domain has been divided into digestible chunks and for each there is a detailed description of the pistes and lifts.

the resort covers the best of the rest of your holiday: a series of reviews on where to eat, where to play, what to do when skiing isn't an option, facilities for children and tips for seasonnaires. Those places that in our opinion deserve a lengthier review are written as a 'feature'.

the a-z comprises a list of tour operators, a directory of contact details (telephone numbers and website addresses) and information from accidents to weather, a glossary of terms used in this guide and in skiing in general, and an index to help navigate your way around the guide.

how to use the maps

The guide also features a number of maps, designed and produced specifically for snowmole. While the information they contain is as accurate as possible, some omissions have been made for the sake of clarity.

route maps   show the journey to the resort from the UK, or from relevant airports or the roads within the area surrounding the resort.

resort maps   for the resort as a whole (showing pedestrianised zones, main buildings, train lines, and road names) and individual maps showing by type the places we review.

ski maps   each individual area has its own contoured map. These show details such as the lifts, pistes and mountain restaurants. The contours have been mapped to fit an A6 page - few ski areas are perfect rectangles. They are accurate only in relation to the pistes they depict and should not be used for navigation. Pistes are shown only in their approximate path - to make the maps as user-friendly as possible some twists and turns have been omitted. The ski maps are grouped together at the back of the book to make them easy to find and refer to - even with gloves on. There is an overview map on the inside back cover that shows the entire ski domain and how the individual ski maps fit together. The back cover has a flap, which is useful as a page marker for the individual ski maps. In the chapter on the skiing the overview map is reproduced in miniature alongside the descriptions of the individual sectors.

explanation of icons

review headers

name — price rating

relevant icons

☎ 0479 055578
🕐 7:30-10:30am, 4pm-10:30am
✕ traditional savoyarde

p107 b4

← map details: page number, grid reference & map cutout showing type and number reference

basic details

- ☎ - telephone number
- 📠 - fax number
- @ - email address
- W^3 - website address
- 🛏 - number of beds
- 📧 - office address
- 🕐 - opening hours
- ✕ - food type

ski school

- ⛷ - ski lessons
- 🏂 - snowboard lessons
- 👨‍👦 - child-specific lessons
- ♿ - disabled skiing
- 🎿 - specialist courses
- **G** - guides available

hotel

- 🥾 - on-site rental store
- 🚌 - shuttle bus

others

- ✕ - food available
- 🎵 - live music
- 📺 - tv
- 🖱 - internet station(s)
- 🍸 - bar
- • - terrace

resort maps

buildings

- i - tourist office
- lp - lift pass office
- PO - post office
- 🛒 - supermarket
- 🎬 - cinema
- ✝ - church

travel specific

- **P** - parking
- **P̂** - covered parking
- **b** - bus stop
- 🚏 - route specific bus stop

commerce colour coding

- ■ - restaurant (local cuisine)
- ■ - restaurant
- ■ - cafe
- ■ - take-away
- ■ - bar
- ■ - nightclub
- ■ - hotel

route maps

- train line & station
- main road & town
- country borders
- motorway & town
- airport

graphic design by Qanuk Publishing & Design Ltd **Q**

introducing zermatt

overview

Some would argue that Zermatt is the most famous resort in the Alps - even if you don't ski, you've probably heard of this Swiss village or at least of the Matterhorn, the area's most prominent peak. Zermatt can thank Switzerland's best-known rock for its success as a winter and summer resort - it has thrived as a destination for skiers, walkers and climbers since the middle of the 19th Century. And today it is still the appeal of the jagged mountain and the memories of the golden alpine age that puts Zermatt at the top of the list for a winter holiday.

Switzerland's southernmost winter resort lies at an altitude of 1620m in the canton of Valais. The village is tucked at the end of the Vispa valley, just before the Swiss-Italian border. Most visitors approach the village on a small mountain train from Täsch, so the first impression is the train station (Bahnhof) and Bahnhofplatz - a bustling square at the north end of Bahnhofstrasse, the resort's main shopping fare. Although the Matterhorn dominates the skyline, the panorama also boasts 29 other peaks above 4000m, including Switzerland's highest mountain, the Monte Rosa (Dufourspitz in German) at 4634m - combined with the startling icy blue of the numerous glaciers, these create a stunning backdrop to the village. But the eye is always drawn to the tooth-like Matterhorn, adopted (and understandably over-used) as Zermatt's emblem. Standing alone on its horizon at a height of 4478m, wherever you are in the village you feel under its magnetic and domineering shadow.

As building space is limited by the steep-sided valley enclosing the village, Zermatt has a somewhat built-up feel. Despite this, it retains an alpine charm that more recently developed resorts are without, even though some of the contemporary additions to the urban skyline are built to a more modern design. The mixture of new and old puts ramshackle wooden huts supported by stilts and stone slabs side by side with sturdy and imposing hotels and contemporary structures made of metal and glass. Ingenious engineering has overcome the inconvenience of the

overview

steep valley walls. Though not immediately visible to the eye, many of the higher-lying buildings are reached from the valley floor by lift (with disconcertingly deep shafts) - and though to get to them you may feel like you're entering a nuclear bunker (or a sewer), it's better than a long uphill walk. To find the Zermatt of old, follow the cobbled twisted alleyways of Hinterdorf, with its collection of tumbledown *stadels*, some of which still house cattle in the winter. The village is ostensibly car-free, though the plethora of deceptively fast electric cars can be a hazard as they zoom around oblivious to their cargo, be it goods or skiers.

There is a permanent community of 5400 inhabitants, mainly Swiss. The visitors too are mainly Swiss - accounting for about half of the 1 million guests received during the winter months. The English are its third biggest market, after the Germans. Zermatt is a resort that engenders loyalty, and it's not so much a question of 'who', but of 'how old'. The average age of the clientele is significantly older than in other resorts - so much so that the local tourist board regularly holds parties to honour those who have been spending their holiday in the resort for 20 years or more.

snapshot

highs...
29 peaks over 4000m
suitable for non-skiers and skiers
gastronomic cuisine
snow 365 days a year
alpine history

and lows
too many paths and flats for boarders
difficult skiing for beginners
Europe's most expensive lift pass
poorly linked ski areas
convoluted journey to the resort

Hotels and apartments make up the bulk of the accommodation - with over 110 hotels and 1500 apartments (with more of both under construction). The range of chalets is more limited. Accommodation is spread throughout the village, and every location has its advantages and disadvantages. Put simply, it is a choice between quiet and remote, or lively and central. Fortunately, with 3 valley-floor lift stations (the Sunnegga funicular, the Gornergrat train station and the Klein Matterhorn lift station) you shouldn't be too far from one of them wherever you stay.

The further east you go in the Alps, the more important après becomes. Or at least this is true of Zermatt when compared to the post-skiing activity typical of resorts in the Western Alps. Zermatt's après starts on the mountain and carries on in the town until the early hours. On the way down from any of the ski areas above the

overview

village, you will find somewhere to suit your après style, be it a warming hot chocolate or a line-up of stomach churning shots.

For many, a winter holiday in Zermatt is as much about the eating as it is about the skiing. Wherever you are on the mountain or in the resort, you are never far from some fine dining. Much of the cuisine available is influenced by the resort's proximity to Italy, as (fortunately) are many of the wine lists. Oddly given its reputation for Epicurean delights, not a single Michelin star has been bestowed.

If you dream of skiing every day (and who doesn't?), Zermatt is for you - the high altitude and extensive glacial area guarantees year round snow so you can ski each and every day you choose. It is not the biggest ski domain in Europe - the combined Zermatt-Cervinia area has just under 400km of pistes (two thirds of the total kilometrage of France's Trois Vallées) - and the lifts are fewer too. But the vertical descents more than compensate: they are among the longest you will find in Europe. From the village you can reach 3 distinct ski areas - the Rothorn, the Gornergrat and the Klein Matterhorn - each served by its own valley-floor lift station. All have some skiing above 3000m, and as high as 3800m on the Klein Matterhorn, which is also the area with the longest winter season in the Alps. The pistes above the Italian resort of Breuil-Cervinia can be reached from the Klein Matterhorn - skiing over an international border is just another attraction of Zermatt. James Bond eat your heart out.

There is enormous opportunity for off-piste too - though because of the extensive expanse of glaciers, skiing without a guide is not advised. But it's worth hiring one to get far away from the pistes and far into a feeling of total remoteness.

seasonal variations

Predicting the weather in the mountains is always difficult, but seemingly more so in Zermatt. A bank of clouds can sit between the peaks for days - sometimes for so long that some visitors may not believe the Matterhorn exists. And when the wind is ripping across one side of the valley, the other side can be calm and sunny.

temperatures
Generally, December and January are colder than February, March and April. Whatever the month, a cloudless blue sky doesn't mean tropical temperatures - and often it will be warmer when snow is falling. Temperatures can range from as low as -10°C in the resort (and colder up the mountain) on the coldest days to as high as 20°C late in the season when the sun is shining.

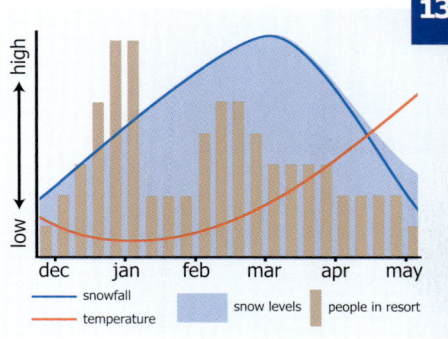

snowfall
Snow depth increases from November through to March at which point it levels off. The best conditions tend to be in February, before the spring sunshine does its damage. Late season snow can fall as low as the village, but tends to melt rather than settle on anywhere but the upper slopes. From mid-March onwards, snow lower down can be patchy and by April it may not be possible to ski all the way home, despite the best efforts of the snow-making machines. That said, the late season skiing is generally more reliable than elsewhere.

volume of people in resort
The number of visitors increases steadily from December to March, with half as many in April and then a healthy population of ski tourers in May. Zermatt is not as susceptible to the half-term influx as other more family-friendly resorts. Like some upmarket French resorts, it is popular with Russian skiers during the first 2 weeks of January for the Russian Christmas and New Year.

quintessential zermatt

Ski resorts are as varied as DNA. But what makes Zermatt Zermatt? To have a quintessential time...

aim high
No other ski resort has mountains in quite the same league - or height - as Zermatt's. First, there is the Matterhorn - the mountain that maketh the resort. And then 29 of Switzerland's 34 peaks over 4000m are in the immediate vicinity, including the highest mountain, Monte Rosa. If you have loftier ambitions, check out what are: the world's highest railway (the Gornergrat); Europe's highest hotel (the Kulmhotel on the Gornergrat 3100m); Europe's highest cable car (the Klein Matterhorn at 3820m); and the highest pisted skiing (winter and summer) in Europe at 3800m from the top of the Klein Matterhorn.

get on your bike
As petrol and diesel cars have been banned from Zermatt since the 1960s, locals have resorted to the humble bicycle to get around. Not the obvious choice, but when in Zermatt... or if that all seems too active (or insane), you can always hail an environmentally friendly, electrically powered car or a horse-drawn carriage. Though there are no stats on how many trainspotters are also skiers, Zermatt has enough trains to satisfy the geek in all of us. They have linked the resort to the outside world - and thankful skiers to the skiing - since the end of the 19th Century.

keep your seat
If you're not the pub crawl type, the something-for-all-people approach of a number of Zermatt's post-ski venues will appeal. The most prolific are the Hotel Post and Vernissage (➥ après-ski & nightlife) - two very different destinations and an example of the extremes of personality, style and design you'll find in the resort. The Post's offerings are housed in Zermatt's third oldest hotel (its date of origin is inscribed on a beam in one of the restaurants). No matter what your leanings,

quintessential zermatt

chances are you will visit the Post (or at least pass by, as it is on Bahnhofstrasse), and the by-line "rooms-restaurants-bars-entertainment" more than adequately sums it up. Vernissage is the new wave and is sought out by those in the know - rather than stumbled across by those who are not. It proposes a more restrained "gallery-cinema-lounge-bar-events" combo, in altogether sleeker surrounds.

feed the locals

Not a charity plea, and the locals in question are cows. Any stale bread you have can be left in the brown Hessian sacks positioned around the village by local farmers.

develop a stomach for heights

Once your head has got used to the altitude, your stomach needs to get used to the food. With close to 40 mountain restaurants - more than the total number of lifts - you can get very used to fine dining with a fine view.

seek divine inspiration

If you need to restore your faith in your technique, the hillside is festooned with almost as many chapels as mountain restaurants. Some are more accessible than others - for most of the year you need skis to get to the Chapel of the Holy Mary of the Snow near Schwarzsee (not ideal if your technique is the reason you're seeking it out). More reachable alternatives include St. Barbara at Zum See, the Chapel of St. James at Findeln, the Chapel of Mary at Blatten, and in addition no fewer than 70 wayside crosses.

learn the hurdy gurdy

Not a dance, but the local lingo - if you suspect the locals of speaking their own language, you're not paranoid, because they are. Known as Zermatter dialect, it is a blend of Swiss-German, Italian and French words and pronunciation. And even if you know some German, you may not recognise some words. For starters, a *buckelpiste* is a mogul field, a *gipfel* is a croissant, *stadels* are stables or small barns and a *stübli* is a homely, casual café.

getting started

planning your trip

Once you know you want to go to Zermatt, you need to decide how you want to get there. Traditionally, most skiing holidays are booked though travel agents or tour operators, but with the advent of cheap flights, DIY holidays are becoming more popular. There are pros and cons to both.

package

The theory behind package holidays is that all you should have to think about is getting from the top of the slopes to the bottom. The core of every package deal is convenience - though it comes wrapped in all kinds of paper. Ski companies fall into 2 types: large mainstream operators, and smaller more specialist ones. The mainstream brand offers ready-made holidays, where everything is already planned and you take it or leave it. Trips with smaller companies can be more expensive, but tend to be more flexible and many tailor the trip to your exact requirements. Alternatively, if you don't want to be restricted to one operator, a travel agent will have access to a selection of holidays offered by several companies.

Mainstream companies only run week-long trips, from Saturday to Saturday or Sunday to Sunday - giving you 6 days on the slopes and 7 nights in (or on) the town. They charter their own **flights** - making the holiday cheaper - but you have little option as to when or from where you travel. Smaller ski companies give you greater choice - many specialise in long weekends for the 'money-rich, time-poor' market, with departures on Thursday evenings and returns on Monday evenings. This gives you 4 days skiing for 2 days off work... but the real advantage is their use of scheduled flights, so you can pick the airport, airline, and when you travel.

With a mainstream company, your **transfer** to resort will be by coach, with others who have booked through the same company. You may have to wait for other flights, and on the way there may be stop-offs in other resorts. Because you're travelling at the weekend the journey tends to take longer. With a smaller company you may transfer by coach, minibus, taxi, or car depending on how much you've paid and the size of your group. And if you arrive mid-week, the transfers tend to be quicker.

What your **accommodation** is depends entirely on whom you book with. Different companies have deals with different hotels, some specialise in chalets... the limiting factor is what's in the brochure - though if you want to stay in a particular hotel, a more specialist company may try to organise it for you.

In **resort** the main benefit of a package holiday is the resort rep. From the moment you arrive to the moment you leave, there is someone whose job it is

planning your trip

to ensure your holiday goes smoothly... or that's the theory. More than likely your rep will sort out lift passes and equipment rental. Some will organise evening activities and be available for a short period every day to answer questions. Most are supported by an in-situ manager who deals with more serious issues. The more you pay for your holiday, the better your rep should be. The best are service-orientated German speakers... but it is difficult to recruit hard-working, intelligent, bilingual people to work for next to nothing. If you want to know what - or who - to expect, ask when you book.

DIY

If you DIY, you have more control over the kind of holiday you take and what you pay. But as you have to make all the arrangements, you'll need more time to plan the trip.

For Zermatt you have the choice of 3 major **airports** - Geneva, Zurich and Milan - and 3 smaller-sized airports - Sion, Basel and Bern. At least 1 airline flies from each of the major UK airports to each of these. As a general rule the traditional airlines (such as BA and Swiss) fly to the major airports and the budget airlines (bmibaby and Easyjet) to the smaller ones (though Easyjet also flies to Geneva). The cheapest flights are normally from London, and the earlier you book the cheaper it will be. The airlines accept reservations for the upcoming winter from around June or July. Some chartered airlines such as Monarch or Thomas Cook airlines may also have a limited number of seats for sale. For **transfers** to Zermatt you have a variety of options (➝ getting there). If you don't want to fly, the excellent European motorway system makes **driving** to the Alps surprisingly easy. Getting there by **train** is also an option.

On a DIY trip the choice of **accommodation** is endless - you are not restricted by brochures or company deals... however the easiest way to book a chalet or an apartment is through a company or website offering accommodation only, such as Interhome or ifyouski.com. You can liaise with the owners directly if you can find their details, but this is often difficult. For hotels you might be able to get a discount off the published price by contacting them directly. For more information on hotels, chalets and apartments ➝ accommodation.

In **resort** is perhaps where the difference between DIY and package is most noticeable. There is no rep on hand so you have to buy your own lift pass, organise your own equipment rental... but this can have its pluses: you can be sure that you get exactly the right type of pass and you can choose which rental shop you use.

getting there

Though for some the journey to Zermatt is part of the fun, it certainly isn't straightforward. It is not close to a major airport, the main road up the valley is a single lane and as the resort is ostensibly car-free, nobody can drive to their accommodation. Once you get to Zermatt you will have to change onto one of the permitted forms of transport - electric car (Zermatt's taxi equivalent), horse drawn sleigh or foot. But the first glimpse of the Matterhorn will make you forget any inconvenience you might feel.

All contact details for the transport listed can be found in the directory.

overland

The most common starting place for any journey by **car** to the Alps is Calais. You can reach Calais from the UK by the **eurotunnel** or **ferry**. Then by car it is just under 1000kms to Zermatt - a journey that can be done in about 11 hours. There are 2 alternatives to the standard **ferry** crossing to Calais. The first is with Norfolkline to Dunkirk - often quieter (and less prone to lorry strikes!) than the Calais services. The second is SpeedFerries.com - a new fast ferry service to Boulogne. SpeedFerries sells tickets on a similar basis to the budget airlines - the earlier you buy, the less you pay.

The journey from Calais takes you east of Paris, through Reims to Dijon, where you branch off to Besançon and cross into Switzerland just before Vallorbe - if you don't have a *vignette* (a windscreen sticker that allows you to use the Swiss motorways) you can buy one here. There are 2 *péage* (toll) stops on the route south through France - you collect a ticket as you enter the motorway and then pay in cash or by credit card as you leave. Expect to pay around €80 in total for the péage and a vignette. If you are stopped and do not have a vignette the police will levy an on-the-spot fine of around CHF100.

The journey continues through Switzerland, mainly by motorway, past the towns of Lausanne, Martigny, Sion and Sierre. The motorway becomes a single lane road just after Sierre. From there follow the signs to Brig/Visp, until you reach the turn-off (from a roundabout) signposted Zermatt - then follow the signs for Zermatt to Täsch and the road's end. This last part of the journey is a winding ascent through the many villages of the Vispa valley.

Cars can only go as far as Täsch (5km from Zermatt), which for this reason resembles a huge car park - with 2,500 open-air and 1,200 indoor spaces. Numerous garages (with indoor or outdoor parking) line the road, or you can park at Täsch's train station. For peak weeks, reserve a parking space well in advance. Alternatively you can leave your car at the train station in Visp and travel the rest of the way by

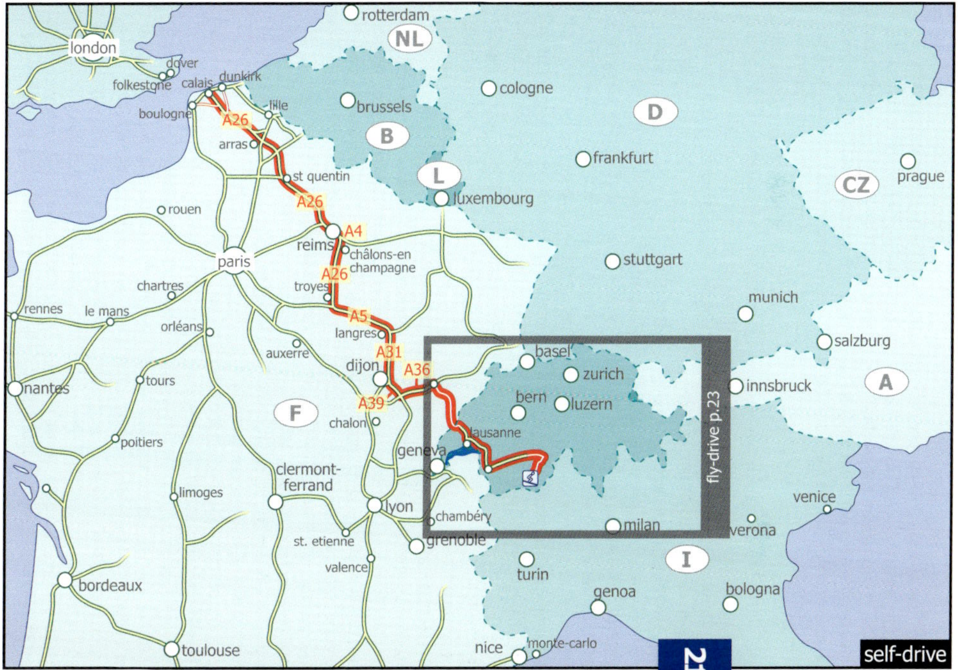

self-drive

21

fly-drive p.23

getting there

train. This parking is free to people using the Visp-Täsch rail service (just make sure you park in the allocated area). The parking fee is reimbursed at the station when you present your car park ticket.

Once you get to Täsch you can carry on by train or taxi. Trains run from Täsch to Zermatt's Bahnhof every 20 minutes 6am-11:30pm and a ticket costs around CHF7 one-way. A taxi can take you as far as the entrance to the resort (minimum charge CHF30), from where you can hail an electric car or complete your journey on foot - though this may involve dragging your luggage some distance through the snow.

If you want to take the train, you can travel to Zermatt on the european **intercity** routes in any number of combinations - via Lille, Strasbourg, Basle... the most logical option is by Eurostar to Paris (Gare du Nord) and from there on the French TGV service from Gare du Lyon to Visp (with a change in Lausanne). Tickets for the Eurostar part of the trip can be booked from July of the preceding summer and it is worth booking ahead, as services become full quickly. The whole journey takes just over 10 hours, and as it is not overnight it does not have the same time-saving attraction of the Snowtrain and Eurostar direct service. These services, however, are not a real option as they only travel French routes from the UK. On the Swiss Rail website (i rail.ch) you can create a train timetable for your journey to Zermatt from your starting point. If you intend to travel on Swiss Rail a number of times during the season, it can be worth investing in a Swiss Pass - a prepaid card for all transportation (trams or buses or trains) in Switzerland. It offer visitors other discounts as well.

by air
Zermatt lies vaguely equidistant between the 3 international **airports** - Geneva, Zurich and Milan. There are daily scheduled flights to each from all major UK airports (➞ planning your trip). The nearest airport to Zermatt is actually Sion, but there are few flights there from the UK.

transfers
How ever you transfer from your arrival airport to Zermatt, you will only get as far as Täsch. The final stage of the journey can be made by train or taxi (as for **overland**) - the Matterhorn remaining tantalisingly hidden from view along the way.

If you want to get to Täsch by **car** you can hire one at any of the airports - by booking over the phone, on the internet or when you arrive. Your car will come with an emergency triangle and, if hired in Switzerland, a motorway vignette - you will need to buy one at the border if you drive from Milan. In every case you should check that it comes with snow

D
basel
A3
A2
A1
zurich
A7
A1
A13
A
FL
A2
A14
A3
luzern
A1
bern
CH
F
A5
A6
A2
flims
klosters
davos
lenzerheide
A12
interlaken
A1
lausanne
gstaad
grindelwald
wengen
st moritz
A1
crans
montana
visp
brig
A2
geneva
sierre
A9
sion
martigny
verbier
täsch
saas-fee
zermatt
chamonix
F
cervinia
I
milan
fly-drive
copyright qanuk 2004

getting there

chains and a roofbox (if you want one). Zermatt lies approximately 135 miles (217kms) from Geneva airport. The journey takes approximately 3 hours - though if you travel at the weekend or during the annual holidays expect traffic and delays. The journey from Sion (70kms) takes about an hour, following the same route as the latter part of the journey form Geneva. It's just under 150 miles (240kms) from Zurich to Zermatt and the journey by car takes on average 4½ hours. There are a variety of routes - if you're not in a rush, the scenic option is a cross-country jaunt through Luzern and Interlaken. From Milan the journey by road (224kms) takes 4 hours. A small toll is payable on the Italian motorway.

The well-known efficiency of the Swiss rail network makes the **train** a hassle-free way to get to Zermatt from any of the airports. From Geneva the journey takes a little longer than by car (3½-4 hours) but gives you time to take in the fantastic scenery along the shores of lake Geneva and then the Rhone valley. There is 1 change, either in Visp or Brig (where you change stations as well as trains). From Zurich the journey takes 5 hours, with a change in Brig and sometimes also in Bern. From Milan the service runs from the Milan Centrale station and also takes 3½-4 hours with a change in Brig. Transfer services run from both Milan airports (Linate and Malpensa) to Milan Centrale station. From Sion it's a 2 hour journey with a change in Visp. And with a service indicative of the ethos of the resort, you can arrange for your luggage to be delivered from Täsch to Zermatt, and to your chosen hotel if you ask nicely (and pay extra). You can book this service until 4pm the day before.

If you don't want to have to worry about driving yourself, there are a number of companies which run **private minibus transfers** from Geneva, Zurich and Milan to Zermatt. Services vary from a simple pick up and drop off to the provision of welcome packs and food and even champagne during your trip. There are a number of services including ATS, Alp Line and Alpine Cab. All of them take online bookings, either via email or direct through the relevant website. You can only book the whole bus, which works out well cost-wise if you are travelling in a large group. If you aren't and want to ensure you have enough personal space you can always take a **taxi**. You don't get the benefit of door-to-door service, and though you do steal a march over the crowds regrouping at Täsch it can only drop you at the entrance to the resort. If you have the money (and a head for heights) transfers by **helicopter** (50 minutes from Geneva, 30 minutes from Milan, 15 minutes from Sion or 1 hour from Zurich) can be organised through Air Zermatt. Remember to travel lightly (or send your bags another way) as luggage space is limited.

getting around

Once you get to Zermatt you only leave the rocky-sided environs of the village to ski and when you depart. Unlike other resorts, all of the skiing ends in the village, so there is no to-ing and fro-ing between other villages or end-points. The village is divided (by name at least) into a number of different districts - though apart from the fairly self-contained Winkelmatten at the south end, the distinction between the start of one area and the end of another is quite blurred. Some parts you are unlikely to visit unless you are staying there. The village as a whole is a maze of narrow streets and pathways, many of which are lined with ropes to make moving down them more of a walk than a slide.

If you think of the village as a long rectangle, split along its length by the glacial waters of the Mattervispa river, you will rarely find yourself lost. You can cross the river at 8 points. While there is accommodation on both sides of the river, the main action takes place on its west bank - concentrated predominantly along Bahnhofstrasse. This is the main street, which runs south to the church square (Kirchplatz). Bahnhofstrasse is the commercial side of Zermatt, and with shops selling many recognisable brands you could as well be on a high street in the UK. If you arrive in Zermatt by train, you come into Bahnhofplatz at the north end of Bahnhofstrasse. The commercial hub is just one face of Zermatt and seems a world away from

snapshot

from zermatt by road to
breuil-cervinia - 6 hours
crans montana - 1 hour 40 mins
saas fee - 1 hour 10 mins
verbier - 2 hours 30 mins
chamonix - 2 hours 40 mins
st. moritz - 5 hours 40 mins

some of the other districts. Weisti (at the north east side of the village) is a quiet and mainly residential area home to the local population and a number of 3* hotels. The oldest houses are found in Oberdorf, towards the Klein Matterhorn lift station. Winkelmatten is the most defined district, having its own small supermarket and a church. Spiss, a pseudo-industrial area at the northernmost extent of the village, is where you will be dropped off if you arrive by taxi (or helicopter!).

There are 3 **valley-floor lift stations**, one for each of the 3 ski areas. The Gornergrat train station (for the Gornergrat area) is the most central - opposite the main Bahnhof. The bottom of the Sunnegga funicular (for the Rothorn slopes) is on the east side of the river, while the Klein Matterhorn lift station (for the Klein Matterhorn pistes and Italy) is at the far south end of the village.

Zermatt's **bus** service is something of a leveller - most people are likely to use it at some point, unless you walk

getting around

everywhere or opt for a taxi. For this reason they can resemble sardine cans during the morning and evening rush hours. The 2 services, use of which is free with your lift pass, operate 7:30am-7pm, both on one-way loops of the village - this may make you feel you are taking a circuitous route to your final destination and in some instances it may be quicker to walk. The green line runs between Spiss and Zen Strecken (the stop for the Klein Matterhorn lift station), while the red line runs between Spiss and Winkelmatten. At the end of the day the queues at Zen Strecken and Winkelmatten can be long - one way to bypass them at Winkelmatten is to wait for the bus opposite the chapel there, before it reaches the main queue one stop further along. Both buses stop at the Bahnhof and the Gornergrat train station, but only the green line stops at the Sunnegga funicular. Otherwise they mostly stop in different places, so make sure you catch the right coloured bus.

If the length of the bus queues leave you frustrated, the alternative way to get around is **on foot**. It is a reasonably short (depending on your view) journey between the far ends of the village (Winkelmatten and Spiss) - about 30 minutes at a brisk pace . Most of the accommodation lies a much shorter distance from one of the valley-floor lift stations. Travelling by **car** is impossible, unless you have your own electrically powered vehicle or a special dispensation from the cantonale police for your petrol or diesel mobile. Unlikely. There are **taxis**, or rather vehicles reminiscent of milk-floats. These operate a similar zoning system to the London's underground, with fixed prices within or across zones. An extra charge is made for luggage - so travel light - and a list of prices is available from the tourist office. Some of the more entrepreneurial drivers operate a different pricing system - they take advantage of the restless many waiting in the long bus queues by filling their cars to capacity, charging a small per-person fee and dropping you wherever you want to go.

If you want a more traditional form of transport you can get around by **horse-drawn carriage** - either to get from 'a' to 'b' or for a spot of sightseeing.

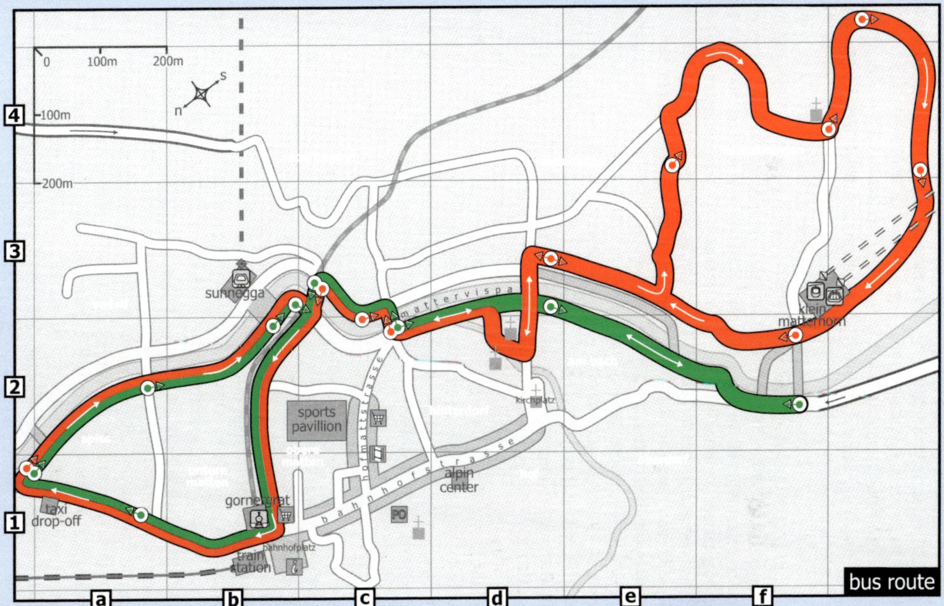

bus route

27

accommodation

At the end of the day on the slopes, you probably won't mind where you rest your head. But when planning your holiday, you might want to put more thought into where you stay.

With over 13,000 tourist beds, Zermatt has plenty of choice - from 5* hotels to 0* hostels, from chalets to private rooms - and there is generally some availability at any time of year. However, if you know where you want to stay, it's best to book early - many of the same visitors return to Zermatt year after year, and often book their accommodation (or preferred room!) a year in advance.

Accommodation - hotels, apartments, private guestrooms and chalets - can be booked through the tourist office, either by telephone or on their website.

hotels

Not the cheapest option - but you can be assured of good service almost without exception. Each hotel has its own character and atmosphere - often the more you pay, the more formal it will be, from the restaurant to the service throughout. The range of hotels in Zermatt is extensive - from the luxurious 5* Riffelalp resort above the village to the 0* YHA. In addition to the standard room rates, many of the hotels offer package deals, which may include lift pass, ski rental or even beauty treatments, or festive week packages (Christmas and New Year) that include gala evenings. All of these can be booked through a tour operator, the tourist office, a travel agent or directly.

As in England, Swiss hotels are graded from 1* to 5* - but here the similarity ends. Stars are awarded for factors such as room size and whether the hotel has a restaurant offering an evening meal. Consequently the facilities one 4* hotel offers can be very different from another, depending upon how it earned its stars. On appearances alone it is often difficult to work out exactly what you'll get - price is generally the best guide.

Some of the hotels are called garnis - and are more akin to a large scale b&b as that is the only type of board available. Hotels proper will offer b&b and half board (and sometimes full board) and a wider range of facilities. Some of the hotels also have 'residences' - apartments equipped for self-catering, though you can still make use of the hotel facilities.

If you want to stay in a hotel and haven't booked before you arrive, there is an information board at the entrance to the train station and another inside the tourist office. These display information about hotel availability and have a free phone from which you can then call your chosen hotel. But a warning - leaving it until you arrive can be a bit of a gamble in high season.

accommodation

specifics

Big or small? Old or new? Whether your taste is for service on tap or taps that need servicing, the hotels we review are those worthy of special mention. Unless otherwise stated, all bedrooms have an en-suite (shower or bath).

Only the hotels actually on the mountain are **ski in/ski out**. Most hotels lie within a short walk of at least one of the 3 valley-floor lift stations, but because of the sprawling nature of the village and the layout of the lift system, no hotel is ideally placed for everything. **availability** is best at the start and end of the season. During the peak weeks the hotels will only take week long **bookings** either Saturday to Saturday or Sunday to Sunday. Over Christmas and New Year, some will only accept 10 or 14 day bookings. Outside of these periods it is possible to book a shorter stay, although you are more likely to get a long weekend if you book last-minute.

In some of the 4* and 5* hotels, **smart dress** is required to dine in the restaurant. For gala evenings (such as at New Year) jacket and tie can be compulsory for men. Many hotels have a deal with a specific rental shop - they will advise you of this when you check in. Every front-of-house employee will speak **english**, so you won't have to rely on your talent for the Zermatterhof dialect. As no cars are allowed into the resort, all must be parked lower down the valley, normally at Täsch. Most of the hotels have a preferred **garage** - from where they will organise your transfer to Zermatt - and will add the price of the parking to your final bill. Most of the hotels also have their own electric car (the more upmarket have a horse-drawn carriage or liveried coach) to pick you up and drop you back at the train station or taxi rank at the

> ### snapshot
>
> ### a seiler of approval
> The Seiler family hotel empire began in 1855 with the purchase of the Monte Rosa. Since then the Mont Cervin, the Schweizerhof and the Nicoletta have been added to the portfolio, in addition to a partnership with the Riffelalp resort. The ethos of the group is good service and this is something you can be assured of at all of the hotels.
>
> Guests staying at any of the hotels can dine at any of the other hotels or restaurants owned by the family. This gives you a choice of 12 - from French country cuisine to sushi - and makes the half board option far more interesting than normal. Book before 12pm the day you want to eat. The hotels also share other services - such as the Mont Cervin's swimming pool - so you can choose the hotel which suits you best and still benefit from facilities elsewhere. An altogether bigger package deal.

accommodation

beginning and end of your stay. Some don't charge you, others do, but very few will shuttle you around the resort for any other reason.

prices

Hotels are divided into 3 price categories - what you can expect to pay for a double room per night in high season, including tax but not service.

luxury - above CHF 400
mid-range - CHF 200-400
budget - below CHF 200

Within these categories, most hotels also have low, mid and high season rates. Prices rise in peak weeks and are at their lowest at the beginning and end of the season. Some have a Christmas/New Year band as well, when prices are at their highest. All hotels accept most credit cards.

snapshot

best for...
liveliness - alex
on a shoestring - bahnhof
peace & quiet - riffelalp resort (2222m)
luxury - zermatterhof
history - monte rosa
heights - schönegg
value for money - biner
families - nicoletta

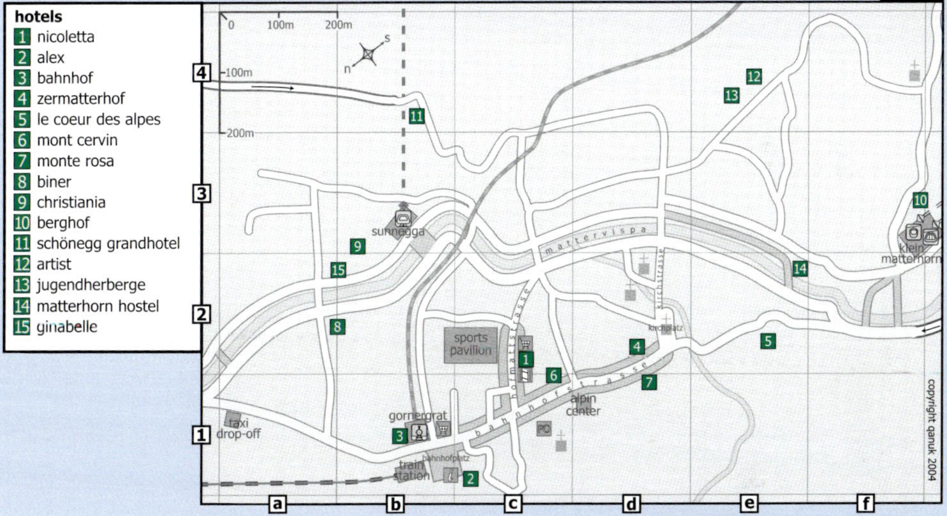

hotels

1. nicoletta
2. alex
3. bahnhof
4. zermatterhof
5. le coeur des alpes
6. mont cervin
7. monte rosa
8. biner
9. christiania
10. berghof
11. schönegg grandhotel
12. artist
13. jugendherberge
14. matterhorn hostel
15. ginabelle

copyright qanuk 2004

31

accommodation

le coeur des alpes****

☎ 027 966 4080
📠 027 966 4081
@ coeurdesalpes@rhone.ch
W³ coeurdesalpes.ch
🛏 14 (b&b)

Le Coeur des Alpes is the new face of Zermatt's hotel scene. It straddles the mid-range/luxury price bracket, but feels closer to the latter. Very much a 'design hotel', it may not be to the taste of traditionalists, but it wouldn't be out of place in a trendy district of London or Paris. Distinctive both inside and out, the architecture and style - a contemporary blend of blond wood, metal and glass - is a departure from the wooden chalet style buildings the Alps and Zermatt are more typically known for.

Perched on a hillside at the southern end of the village near the Klein Matterhorn lift station, it sits in a noticeable enclave with its similarly designed neighbours - the View House and the Casa Vanessa Aparthotel. Fortunately the hotel can be reached from the lower levels by lift. The communal areas and bedrooms feature pieces from Heinz Julen's distinctive furniture collection (➥ '57 ways to decorate a room?'). The most unusual fitting hangs from the ceiling in the reception area - a metal fireplace suspended over a glass floor, which overlooks a monochrome tiled jacuzzi on the floor below. The hotel's window cleaner has an unenviable task as glass is put to good use throughout - large picture book windows make the most of the hotel's hilltop vantage spot. The penthouse has a ceiling made of glass so you can bask in the alpine sunrays, or enjoy a blizzard from the comfort of the indoors. The bedrooms on lower floors have less transparent ceilings, but nonetheless are spacious and light, all having balconies and half having a Matterhorn view.

accommodation

<< luxury >>

mont cervin***
- 027 966 8888
- 027 966 8899
- @ montcervin@zermatt.ch
- W³ seilerhotels.ch/montcervin
- 128 (b&b/½/full)

p31 c1/2 — 6

One of the 4 hotels owned by the Seiler family (→ 'a seiler of approval'), the Mont Cervin is the 5* offering in the portfolio. The granddaddy of the group in terms of size, it is grand in most other ways too - furnishings, service, guests. Its central location on Bahnhofstrasse puts it at the heart of the resort - the courtyard terrace at the front is a serene setting from which to watch the hoi polloi. If you want 5* surroundings but 1* interaction with the other guests the hotel also has a residence with 15 spacious apartments - connected by a passage underneath the main street. And those wondering from which peak the hotel takes its name need only ask a Frenchman.

zermatterhof***
- 027 966 6600
- 027 966 6699
- @ info@zermatterhof.ch
- W³ zermatterhof.ch
- 84 (b&b/½)

p31 d2 — 4

If the Mont Cervin is the Granddaddy, the Zermatterhof is the Grande Dame. Built in 1879, it is a throwback to the Zermatt of old and a reminder of how things used to be done. And done properly - the Zermatterhof does most things by the luxury-lined book. As it sits in the grounds of a private park it even has the luxury of space - a sought-after commodity in short-on-space Zermatt. A recent extension makes it home to Zermatt's only casino, adding to the rather glitzy feel and the overriding feeling that you need money to stay here. This is a hotel for those who like their service to be on the starched side of formal and the price to be reassuringly expensive.

riffelalp resort***
- 027 966 0555
- 027 966 0550
- @ reservation@riffelalp.com
- W³ riffelalp.com
- 63 (b&b, ½)

The Riffelalp resort sits (2222m) high on a plateau above the village, on the Gornergrat ski area, near the Riffelalp

33

accommodation

train station. The hotel will collect you on a blanket-covered sleigh for the short journey to the hotel along a forest path lit with Narnian lamp posts - so don't forget to take some Turkish delight. The Riffelalp is a self-sufficient "resort hotel" - it has its own ski shops, 2 restaurants, a piano bar, a small cinema, a games room, a pool and fitness suite, a wine cellar and even its own mountain guide. Bedrooms are divided between the old hotel and a new annexe, the furnishings reflecting which building you are in - floral and dark wood ("Nostalgie") in the old and pale colours and light wood ("Chalet") in the new. While for some the hotel's remoteness is one of the main attractions, those who need reassurance that there is life outside the palatial surroundings will be relieved that trains run every hour (ish) until 12pm between the hotel and Zermatt.

monte rosa★★★★

p31 d1 — 7

☎ 027 966 0333
📞 027 966 0330
@ monterosa@zermatt.ch
W³ seilerhotels.ch/monterosa
🛏 47 (b&b/½)

As Zermatt's original tourist accommodation (a 3-room hostel called the Lauber Inn, which first opened to residents in 1839) the Monte Rosa takes pride of hotel place in the resort's history books. And proud of its history it is - a bronze plaque on the outside records that Edward Whymper's expedition up the Matterhorn in the 1850s (the first successful one) started here. Though the hotel has been much extended since, original features have been well preserved - charmingly uneven floors lead to cosy rooms, including a sun-lit snug on the first floor that pays homage to past guests and the golden age of alpinism. While the Zermatterhof opposite is about fur-coated glamour, the Monte Rosa is about understated elegance.

<< mid-range >>

alex★★★★

p31 c1 — 2

☎ 027 966 7070
📞 027 966 7090
@ info@hotelalexzermatt.com
W³ hotelalexzermatt.com
🛏 67 (b&b/½)

One of Zermatt's more eclectic hotels, the Alex's individuality has secured it a large fan-base. A 'more is more' approach has been taken to the interior - no surface (ceilings included) has escaped without rather lavish rather romantic embellishment. This theme continues in the bedrooms, which have intensely floral furnishings and four-poster beds (and fireplaces) in some. The leisure facilities are excellent and include a pillared swimming pool somewhat reminiscent of a Roman bath. The hotel is close to Bahnhofstrasse, and the heart of resort life, but it is far enough away for its immediate

accommodation

surroundings to be serenely quiet. Except at night, when the in-house disco warms up - expect oldies (clientele and records). Should the fan-base have booked before you, the owners also run the Schlosshotel Tenne (t 027 966 4400, i reconline.ch/tenne) - a castle-like hotel near the Gornergrat train station.

biner***

- 027 966 5666
- 027 966 5667
- @ info@hotel-biner-zermatt.ch
- w³ hotel-biner-zermatt.ch
- 48 (b&b/½)

p31 a/b2 — 8

The one hotel in Zermatt that makes you question the way in which stars are awarded - the Biner is an underrated (3) star. Hard to beat for location, it sits on a quiet corner overlooking the Mattervispa river within an easy 5 minute walk of both the Sunnegga funicular and the Gornergrat train station, and within yodelling distance of Bahnhofstrasse. The loft-style rooms on the top floor (some with a Matterhorn view) are the most desirable, though recent renovations have transformed the hotel as a whole into a blond-wooded, white-walled refuge. And few 3* spots have comparable leisure facilities - a pool, jacuzzi, sauna and thermal bath complex in the basement. In the lobby-restaurant-bar area, the main attraction is a collection of hammocks that, like haribo, are enjoyed by both big and small.

christiania****

- 027 966 8000
- 027 966 8010
- @ christiania.zermatt@reconline.ch
- w³ reconline.ch/christiania
- 72 (b&b/½)

p31 b3 — 9

Both a hotel and a garni - made up of 2 neighbouring buildings, to make up one of Zermatt's biggest hotels. One can be reached from the other down a long corridor over the Christiania's best feature - an enormous swimming pool (free to all guests). The corridor also prevents those staying in the garni from having to brave the elements to get to the central reception, and the Christiania's restaurant and main bar, which are all in the hotel. Breakfast is the only time big isn't beautiful, as all guests descend on the relatively small and badly arranged breakfast room in the hotel, meaning it can be a bit of a scrum for the milk. Over half the rooms have a Matterhorn view and the Sunnegga funicular is a 2 minute walk away.

berghof****

- 027 967 5400
- 027 967 5452
- @ info@berghof-zermatt.ch
- w³ berghof-zermatt.ch
- 28 (b&b/½/full)

p31 f3 — 10

"Herzlich Willkommen" is what it says above the door and heartily welcomed is how you will feel at this family-run hotel

accommodation

close to the Klein Matterhorn lift station. The chalet-style architecture and warm décor give it an air of informality that other 4* are often without. It is well laid out throughout, with a number of well-placed fireplaces to defrost in front of and comfortable seating to sink into at the end of the day. All bedrooms have balconies, some have their own fireplace or four-poster bed. The swimming pool and wellness area are an important part of the operation - the hotel offers a relaxation package, perfect for those who would rather make more of the on-site facilities than those outside.

schönegg grandhotel****

p31 b4 | 11

☎ 027 967 4488
📠 027 967 5808
@ schonegg.zermatt@reconline.ch
W³ reconline.ch/schonegg
🛏 37 (b&b/½)

In a resort with so many 4* hotels, it can be difficult to decide between them. And at first glance the Schönegg is on a par with the rest - same range of facilities, same pleasant surroundings. Its USP is that it is the only 4* hotel within walking (or actually lift) distance of the village that you can also reach on skis - the blue piste home from the Rothorn ski area passes by the front door. And its elevated position high up the valley sides give it a further advantage - an unrestricted view of the Matterhorn… should you be worried about not seeing it.

<< budget >>

artist***

p31 e4 | 12

☎ 027 966 2900
📠 027 966 2905
@ tannegg@zermatt.ch
W³ artistapartments.ch
🛏 10 (b&b)

The appropriately named Artist pays homage to the world of painters and daubers. Every room is decorated in the style of a well-known artist, from a bleak Edward Hopper to a more up-beat Pablo Picasso. In addition all rooms have a small kitchenette, a balcony and a Matterhorn view, making the price even more of a bargain - the last being something not all hotels with more stars can offer. Rooms can be hired on a garni or an apartment basis - breakfast is available or you can ask the friendly staff to order bread in for you should you want to make your own.

bahnhof

p31 b1 | 3

☎ 027 967 2406
📠 027 967 7216
@ welcome@hotelbahnhof.com
W³ hotelbahnhof.com
🛏 17 (bed only)

The observant won't be surprised that this hotel is located opposite the main train station and next door to the Gornergrat train station. More of a hostel than a hotel, only beds are on offer.

accommodation

Rooms range from singles to dormitories, with or without an en-suite bathroom. If a wish on your holiday list is that somebody else makes your breakfast, it is not the place for you, but it does have a kitchen for those able to pour their own cornflakes. With its central location, it's a good option if you don't want to invest in somewhere for your luggage.

jugendherberge (YHA)

p31 e4 | 13

☎ 027 967 2320
📞 027 967 5306
@ zermatt@youthhostel.ch
W³ youthhostel.ch/zermatt
🛏 174 (b&b/½/full)

Towards the south end of the village and Winkelmatten, Zermatt's YHA contradicts existing stereotypes about youth hostels. Housed in 3 buildings, it was renovated and refurbished recently, and is now more modern, cleaner and more comfortable than some more stellar places - which makes it an option for those who are some way from being 'youths'. Bedrooms range from twin rooms to 8 bed dorms and most have en-suite facilities - and a number of them have Matterhorn views. The price includes a buffet breakfast and an evening meal (with a packed lunch available on request and for extra francs). Other facilities include an internet connection and a games corner for those non-skiing days.

matterhorn hostel

p31 e2 | 14

☎ 027 968 1919
📞 027 968 1915
@ info@matterhornhostel.com
W³ matterhornhostel.com
🛏 10 rooms (56 beds)

On the floor above the Dorfbeizli restaurant (➙ eating out), the Matterhorn hostel is housed in a charming chalet-style building. Sadly this charm isn't as obvious on the inside - the focus switches to necessities, of a fairly bare kind. Beds are available in rooms of 2-8 - perfect for those who want to get close and cosy with their room-mates. But it's not the place for your cat, as you won't be able to swing it.

and the rest

If you want to look down on the rest - or just be the first to spoil the work of the piste bashers - the options on the **mountain** include the Bärghüs Grünsee (t 027 967 2553, i zermatt.ch/gruensee) at 2300m near Gant and the Schwarzee (t 027 9667 2263) at 2600m at Schwarzsee. For **good food** one of the best hotel restaurants is the Schäferstübli at the 4* Julen (t 027 966 7600, i julen.com). One menu is totally lamb-based (except dessert), using animals reared on its own breeding farm. The 4* Daniela (t 027 966 7700, i zermatt.ch/daniela) is owned by the same family. The 4* Albana Real (t 027 966 6161, i hotelalbanareal.com) is home to a Japanese and a Thai

37

restaurant (Fuji and Rua Thai respectively) (➥ eating out). For hotels catering best for **kids** ➥ children. **bahnhofstrasse** is lined with hotels and garnis for those not wanting to miss out - options include the 2* Burgener (t 027 967 1020, i rhone.ch/hotelburgener), the 3* Darioli (t 027 967 2748, i darioli.ch) and the 4* Walliserhof (t 027 966 6555, i reconline.ch/walliserhof). A number of hotels have **swimming pools** on-site for those who like to get in a few lengths before breakfast - try the 4* Parkhotel Beau-site (t 027 966 6868, i parkhotel-beausite.ch) and the 4* Eden garni (t 027 967 2655, i hotel-eden.ch).

chalets

Chalet holidays cater for those who want to stay in a more relaxed setting, but don't want to fend for themselves.

tour companies

As only a handful of UK tour companies (➥ tour operators) operate in Zermatt, a typical chalet holiday is less easy to come by than in some other resorts. And there are few 'chalets' in the ideal sense of the word - most turn out to be part of a larger building rather than a chocolate box whole. Despite the scarcity, the typical package - bed, breakfast, afternoon tea and on 6 nights out of 7 an evening meal with wine - is available. You will be looked after by at least one English chalet host and a resort rep. The more mainstream operators also organise flights and transfers and some offer discounts to big groups and families. The rule of thumb is that the more you pay, the better you can expect the quality of everything to be. But unless you book the whole place you take pot luck with your fellow guests - it can be a war-zone or the beginning of a beautiful friendship - but at least you know you all like snow.

independents

Information on privately-run chalets is not as easy to find, although the internet is a good place to start - some owners have their own websites or list their chalets on sites such as ifyouski.com. What is on offer in

accommodation

privately run chalets varies greatly. Some provide a similar package to those run by tour companies, some are bed & breakfast only, and in some you are left entirely to your own devices. One of the few detached chalets in Zermatt is the tiny Chalet Yukon (t 027 967 1620), a dinky little building opposite the Klein Matterhorn lift station, which sleeps a maximum of 3 people.

aparthotels

Aparthotels are an apartment/hotel hybrid, the German equivalent of a French *résidence* - they provide the facilities and comforts of a hotel, without staff waiting in the shadows to answer your every need. Zermatt has a number, including the **zurbriggen** (t 027 966 3838, i zurbriggen.ch) owned by one of its sons-by-marriage, Pirmin Zurbriggen, the former downhill skier. Located just beyond the Klein Matterhorn lift station, it sets the aparthotel standard. Warmly decorated throughout with muted colours and pale wood, it is also exquisitely furnished - thanks to Zurbriggen's brother-in-law Heinz Julen (➜ '57 ways to decorate a room?'). The route of the Matterhorn Express gondola is over the aparthotel, so if you want a look, you can get a bird's eye view of the rooms.

The **casa vanessa** (t 027 966 3510, i casavanessa.ch) slightly further down the road from the Zurbriggen (and next door to Le Coeur des Alpes hotel) is in

> ### snapshot
>
> **57 ways to decorate a room?**
> The resort is a showcase for the talents of Heinz Julen, a local boy and a well known interior designer. His range of signature furniture and light fittings can be seen everywhere, decorating many of the bars and restaurants including Vernissage and Mood's (➜ après-ski & nightlife). He has also helped to style and design some of the hotels and aparthotels, including one for himself. Julen and his wife own the **view house** (t 079 235 1727, i viewhouse.ch), next door to the Casa Vanessa aparthotel and Le Coeur des Alpes hotel (➜ hotels). A luxurious development of 4 "dwellings", this is apartment living at top class hotel standards. Built out of wood, metal and glass, each apartment is beautifully furnished with Julen designed pieces and art. Each apartment sleeps 4 comfortably and and each is decorated in an individual colour theme - a vibrant blue, a sunny yellow, a bright red or a more calming green - so there is something to suit all wardrobes.

the same vein. Immaculately furnished, there is a well-equipped fitness suite and some of its apartments have their own fires and a Matterhorn view - the latter being the not-so-unique selling point of much of Zermatt's accommodation.

accommodation

apartments

Ski apartments are typically compact and bijoux. But Zermatt isn't a typical ski resort and with over 1500 apartments to choose from, it is inevitable that some don't quite fit the stereotype. True, some provide the basic roof and 4 walls, but others are luxurious in the extreme, such as the charming **annapurna** close to the Sunnegga funicular and the familialy owned **la cordée** by the Klein Matterhorn lift station (t 027 967 2851, i lacordee.ch). Both contain such luxuries as dishwashers and internet connection. The former has a wellness suite and at the latter "well-educated and happy" pets are welcome.

Apartments are not uniformly graded and there are a number of classifications in use. The Swiss Tourist Board uses a star classification - this is based on the facilities available, but tends to reflect whether or not there is a shoeshine machine rather than providing an indication of the level of comfort you can expect. Facilities do differ. Some (in addition to the standard accommodation) have a swimming pool and/or a sauna and jacuzzi - such as the **paradies** apartment block (t 027 966 2480, i zermatt.ch/paradies). Wherever you stay you can expect to be provided with kitchen facilities and utensils, along with bed linen and a simple cleaning kit. In the most basic apartments this means a fridge, a hob, pots and pans, a few knives and forks and some washing-up liquid. Another indication of quality is the local ZAV-Quality mark - a group of Zermatt landlords formed the organisation to guide visitors to the quality of the accommodation available (Zermatt Apartment Verein t 027 966 8100, i zermattapartment.com). Various requirements have to be fulfilled to become a member - primarily landlords have to classify their apartments on a 1*-5* basis and comply with the ZAV criteria and guidelines.

Because of the number of apartments, the tourist office does not publish a comprehensive list, although it keeps records of most (they will provide details over the phone or you can find them on their website). You can use this information to contact the owners directly or book through the tourist office. Or you can use one of the accommodation agencies, though they will charge a booking fee. **interhome** has an office in Zermatt, just off Bahnhofplatz (t 027 967 3654, i interhome.ch) and keeps details of over 60 privately-owned apartments of varying size and price to choose from. Some tour companies will source accommodation-only apartments for you.

Apartments are on the face of it the cheapest place to stay - but when you add in the price of eating, either in or out, you can pay more overall than you would if you were staying in a chalet or a hotel. However, if you can stay

accommodation

disciplined about what you spend on food (a challenge in Zermatt), it can be a cost-effective holiday. Prices vary depending upon whether it is high, mid or low season. As a guide, a short-term let for a mid-grade apartment with 2 bedrooms costs approximately CHF2800 in peak weeks and CHF1200 in low season.

Some apartments are available on a long-let if you want a place for the season. The demand is high, so you need to start looking in the summer before the season starts.

Another way to stay in an apartment is to book a **matterhorn ski week** (*matterhorn skiwochen*) (t 027 966 2461, i matterhornskiwochen.ch). Available during low season only, 'weeks' are a package deal which include your apartment (or hotel if you prefer), ski instruction, ski rental and a lift pass.

private rooms

A limited number of private rooms - doubles and singles - are available within privately owned houses. These are generally good value and give an option to lone travellers reluctant to pay a single person's supplement. The tourist office keeps a list of those available.

camping

Yes, really - there is a winter campsite down the valley in the village of Randa. If the idea of camping in winter is not off-putting enough you also have to take the Täsch-Zermatt-Täsch train every day to get to and from the skiing. Only recommended for those made of truly stern stuff.

lift passes

Once you've arrived in Zermatt and found where you're staying, there are a few things to sort out before you can get onto the slopes. For many people, long queues and language barriers make this the worst part of the holiday. Starting with lift passes, the following pages take you step by step through the process and how to survive it.

> **snapshot**
>
> **useful information**
> hands-free system
> no photo required
> refundable deposit
> generous discount for children
> winter peak pass for walkers

Zermatt's lift pass system is as state-of-the-art as you will find. The resort has been using an electronic checking system (Skidata) since 1999. With this system, the lift pass of your chosen duration and area is loaded onto a re-usable credit-card sized piece of plastic - for which you pay a refundable deposit of CHF5. This is scanned at the entry point to each lift - you don't even have to take it out of your pocket. Nor do you need to take a photo - each lift pass office has a small desk-top camera with which to take a mug-shot. Lift passes can also be loaded onto swatch watches that have the ski data system.

1 or 2 countries?

Once you've decided how many days, the other, rather more glamorous decision you have to make is whether you will limit your skiing to Switzerland or whether you will venture into Italy. The lift pass covering Zermatt and Breuil-Cervinia is the more expensive of the two and is called Skipass International. The pass for Zermatt only is called Skipass Zermatt. Both passes include the use of the buses around the resort. If you are going to buy a lift pass for 6, 7, 13 or 14 days, another option is the International-Aosta skipass. Only available for those durations (and more expensive than the International Pass), it means you can venture further into Italy. If you intend to ski in Italy, don't forget to take your passport with you. And don't bring back too much duty free - look out for the customs controls.

handy to know

The lift system is run by Zermatt Bergbahnen. Main lift pass offices are located at the bottom of the Sunnegga funicular, the Gornergrat train station, the Klein Matterhorn lift station and the train station at Täsch. You can also buy passes from the Alpin Center on Bahnhofstrasse (open Mondays to Saturdays 8am-11:30am, 3pm-7pm and Sundays 8am-11:30am, 4pm-7pm). Some hotels will organise passes for you - particularly if you buy them as part of a inclusive package.

Zermatt offers one of the most generous **discounts** that you will find in the Alps - **children aged 9** years or

lift passes

below are entitled to a free ski-pass. Otherwise, the discounts available are fairly standard - children aged **10-16** (inclusive) only pay 50% of the price for a pass and those aged **16-21** qualify for a 15% discount, as do skiers aged **65 or older**. Perhaps because of the nature of the skiing, there is no beginners pass.

A **half-day** pass (marginally cheaper) can be bought on the day of intended use from 12:15pm onwards. **day** passes are available as well, but if you intend to ski every day for a stretch of time, it is more cost-effective to buy a pass for the full length of time you intend to ski. If your stay is for 7 days, but you know you won't ski every day, you can buy a pass that lets you ski 5 days (your choice) out of the 7 (or for longer stays, 8 days out of 10 and 11 days out of 13).

A good option for walkers - or non-skiers who want to admire the view - is the **winter peak pass**. This gives unlimited access to all lifts suitable for non-skiers in the Zermatt area, giving you the opportunity to visit the viewpoints of the 3 ski areas. You can also buy this type of pass for 3 days out of 5 or 4 days out of 6. This pass is free for children under 6 and those aged between 6-16 qualify for a 50% discount. You can pay for a one-way or return trip on several of the gondolas and cable cars as well as the Sunnegga funicular and Gornergrat train. Prices vary from lift to lift, children qualify for a discount, and if you have a Swisspass (➝ getting there), you are entitled to a discount. Groups of 10 or more also get cheaper price tickets. Those staying in Zermatt for longer than the typical 1 week can buy a pass for a month, a season or a year - depending upon how lucky you are. If you intend to try out skiing in a bikini there is also a **summer skiing** lift pass.

For any of the discounted or special passes you need to show proof of age at purchase. Passes are not transferable - if you don't have one, or you have one that is not yours, you can be fined.

Personal **insurance** against accidents on the slopes is not included with your lift pass. If you have not organised your own cover before your arrive in Zermatt, you can buy an Air Zermatt card. This card is good throughout Switzerland for 1 year and covers the cost of any assistance you need for on-piste incidents, including blood-wagon and helicopter recovery. Personal and family cards are available.

skis, boots & boards

The approach to equipment rental is not (yet) quite as radical as that in resorts such as Courchevel or Val d'Isère. In Zermatt you still have to go to the shop to try on your boots and choose your skis. Some shops take the sting out of it slightly, with online reservation systems or a delivery service to and from your accommodation once you have chosen what you want. As with buying your lift pass, if you avoid Saturdays and Sunday mornings, typically the busiest times, you shouldn't have to wait for hours.

handy to know
Getting the right **equipment** will ensure you fully enjoy your holiday. Your feet will hurt if you don't get well-fitting boots so don't be embarrassed to persevere until you find a pair that fits. If they cause you problems on the slopes, take them back - all the shops will help you find a more suitable pair. Unless you know you want a specific type or make of ski, take the advice of the ski fitter. They are the experts and will know which is the best ski for you based on your ability and age.

Though the range of equipment is extensive, conversely to the French resorts it's easy to get hold of skis made by Stöckli, Fischer and Völkl but less easy to find Atomics, Salomons and Rossignols. A 6-day ski and boot package is on average CHF270 for adults and CHF130 for children. Most of the shops are open all day (8am-7pm) on a Saturday but close for lunch on every other day.

At most shops you can take out **insurance** (except on test skis) to cover accidental breakage, loss or theft. Skiing on roads is not insurable! Unfortunately skis do get stolen or taken by accident - with so many people using the same makes it's easy to confuse your skis with those belonging to somebody else. When you stop for lunch or après it's a good idea to swap one of your skis with a friend so you both have a mis-matched pair. This helps to ensure that nobody will pick up your skis, either by mistake or otherwise.

for skis
bayard (part of the swissrentasport chain) has 3 stores in Zermatt (and 1 at the Riffelalp resort). Its main store and the largest of the three is opposite the Bahnhof. It stocks a wide range of rental equipment - alpine skis, some snowboards and touring equipment - and has a large locker area where you can store equipment rented from any of the Bayard stores. You can reserve your equipment before you arrive in resort on their website (i bayardzermatt.ch). There is another, smaller Bayard store further up Bahnhofstrasse. The third store is beside the Bahnhof and specialises in technical clothing, such as Arc'teryx and Mammut. If you intend to revisit the Swiss Alps more than once in a season you can buy a card

skis, boots & boards

("PassePartout") for CHF 600 which entitles you to rent your choice of equipment from any of the other swissrentasport shops during any of your visits.

For those adverse to lugging equipment around, **burgener sport** on Bahnhofstrasse will deliver your skis to your accommodation and pick them up at the end of your stay.

flexrent has 2 outlets, both conveniently located near a main lift station: one (Dorsaz Sports) is at the Klein Matterhorn lift station and the other (Flexrent) is opposite the Sunnegga funicular. You can leave your equipment overnight in the stores for free. If you rent from Dorsaz and then decide you will start your skiing the next day from the Sunnegga funicular the shop will transfer your skis to its other store overnight. And vice versa. Dorsaz also has a huge service centre.

for boots

The Canadians and their boot-fitting technology haven't made it this far east in the Swiss Alps yet, but one American has. Bill Baker at **julen sport** on Hofmattstrasse has been based there for over 15 years and has an excellent reputation for his craft. He works with computer designed footbeds - worth considering if you have problem feet or want a performance fit.

for boards

Most of the ski rental shops, but not all, stock boards and only 1 store - **julen sport** - has a truly dedicated board section. Run in partnership with the Stoked Snowboard School (➜ lessons & guiding), it offers a wide range of boards for sale or rental (including Burton, Nitro, Salomon and Santa Cruz) as well as accessories, and it does servicing and repairs.

If you want Flow bindings, go to one of the 3 **matterhorn sport** (matterhornsport.ch) outlets: its main one on Bahnhofstrasse, one opposite the Biner hotel on Matterstrasse and one by the hotel Aristella on Steinmattstrasse.

for other equipment

Rental shops also stock a wide range of ski clothing - although brands differ from shop to shop so you will need to search around if you are looking for a specific make - as well as all the accessories you can think of. There is little difference from what you would pay for the same clothes in the UK.

Some shops have a particular speciality. **anorak** on Bahnhofstrasse only deals with telemark and touring skis. You can also hire an avalanche pack (transceiver, shovel and probe) from here, as well as from the main Bayard store opposite the train station. Any of the Matterhorn Sport shops will also hire out avalanche transceivers.

lessons & guiding

ski schools

Zermatt only has 2 ski schools - the Swiss Ski & Snowboard School (SSS) and Stoked. Both are Swiss-run and both are "official" - whilst in France the ESF is (tacitly) promoted by the tourist offices, in Switzerland all ski schools have equal standing.

handy to know

The cheapest way to learn to ski is in **group lessons**. When you book you will be asked your level of skiing so you can be put with a group of skiers of a similar standard to yours. Stoked splits its classes into 5 levels, and the SSS into 6. Generally where you belong depends upon the colour of piste you are comfortable skiing on or your own assessment of your overall standard of skiing. As a guide, level 1 is for complete beginners, level 3/4 for skiers who can do parallel turns on blue pistes and level 5/6 for good skiers in all conditions. In practice the divisions are not as accurate as they could be - some people overestimate their ability or misunderstand words like 'confident' and 'controlled', so to an extent the level of your group is pot luck. As long as you can distinguish whether you are a beginner, an intermediate, or an advanced skier, you are likely to find yourself in roughly the right place. Group lessons at both schools last for 5 hours.

If you have the money, **private lessons** are without question the way forward. Once you're past the basics, individual attention is the best way to significantly improve your technique and is often better value. If you can get a group of 4 or more the individual price per day is similar to the average price per day for group lessons, with the advantage that you go where you want to go and practise what you want to practise. Private lessons can be booked for 2, 3 or 5 hours at both schools or you can opt for the "VIP" service - a full day private lesson, which starts with a pick-up from your hotel - which at least saves you from having to find your instructor in a sea of similarly-clad individuals.

There is some difference in the **cost** of lessons. Stoked's group lessons are significantly more expensive than the same at the SSS (CHF450 v. CHF300). There's little in it for private lessons - as a rough guide, a half-day private lesson for 1 or 2 people costs just under CHF200 and just over CHF300 a full day. You can pay for your lessons in cash or by credit card. The price does not include personal insurance or a lift pass.

Both Stoked and the SSS offer **snowboarding lessons**, again in group or private format. A full day lasts for 4 hours (with a break for lunch) and a half for 2½ hours. In addition, the ISSI (Independent Swiss Snowboard Instructors) only offers snowboarding lessons.

lessons & guiding

children aged 9 and above can join the SSS adult lessons - aged 13 and above at Stoked. For other lessons for kids ➥ children.

Either make your **booking** before you get to Zermatt - by email, fax or phone - or once you're in resort, in person at the ski school office. Always pre-book in peak season, as there are not enough instructors to meet demand - both schools recommend booking at least 2 weeks in advance. To confirm your booking, the schools need your name, level of ability and a credit card number.

Both schools have a number of **meeting points** - the top of the Sunnegga funicular, Trockener Steg, Riffelberg... exactly where will be confirmed when you book. The location for each subsequent day will be decided the day before - so pay attention in class - depending upon snow conditions and the make-up of the group. At the end of the lesson you're on your own.

In Switzerland, ski **instructors** can work without any qualifications. Despite this, the bulk of instructors in Zermatt are Swiss (only a handful are English) - but they should be able to get across how to bend your knees. If you want to ensure you are taught by a qualified instructor ask when you book your lesson. If you hire an instructor for a whole day, it is customary for you to buy them lunch - whether or not you tip is up to you.

Lessons take place **whatever the weather**, unless the entire lift system is closed in which case the schools will refund the full lesson price. They will also refund you if you are ill or have an accident and can produce a valid medical certificate. If you cancel a lesson for any other reason, it must be by 7pm the day before the lesson to get a refund from Stoked and before 5:30pm to get a refund from the SSS.

lessons & guiding

ski & snowboard school

☏ 027 966 2466
✆ 027 966 2464
@ info@skischulezermatt.ch
w³ skischulezermatt.ch
🗐 alpin center

The older of the 2 ski schools (in years and the average age of the instructors) and the one with the greater resemblance to France's ESF. Having a bigger instructor base than Stoked, it is able to offer lessons in more disciplines - including telemark and off-piste lessons. Bizarrely given its bigger instructor base, group lessons tend to have a larger class size (needing a minimum of 6 before they will run them). Lessons run from just before Christmas to the end of April and can be booked at the Alpin Center Mondays to Saturdays 8am-12pm, 3pm-7pm and 8am-12pm, 4pm-7pm on Sundays.

stoked

☏ 027 967 7020
✆ 027 967 7022
@ info@stoked.ch
w³ stoked.ch
🗐 hofmattstrasse

The school with the hipper image, Stoked was established in 1994. Seemingly more concerned with the SSS in ensuring everybody gets enough attention, Stoked promises smaller classes (a minimum of 4 and a maximum of 8 per group). Other strings to its youthful bow include a skate, snowboard and streetwear shop and snowboard rental and sale shop run out of Julen Sport (all on Hofmattstrasse). And if you want to get in some sneaky practise while your skiing rivals are lazing on a beach, Stoked offers private lessons for 2, 3 or 5 hours during the summer months. Lessons (year round) can be booked at their office on Hofmattstrasse 8am-7pm Mondays to Saturdays and 8am-12pm, 3pm-7pm on Sundays. And if you're looking for an English instructor you're more likely to find one here.

issi

☏ 027 967 7067
✆
@ info@issi.ch
w³
🗐 victoria center

A small and well-hidden school (in the Victoria Centre, opposite the Bahnhof), ISSI's speciality is snowboard lessons - private only, for 2 or 3 hours or a full day. They use video analysis so you can see where you are going wrong with your technique. If you would rather be seen dead than with one plank on your feet, they are also happy away from the markers and offer guiding for skiers and telemarkers as well as boarders.

48

lessons & guiding

guides

The view from the village is of a fantastic and endless expanse of snowfields. But the terrain away from the valley's pisted areas is glaciated and so is life threatening to the ignorant. To experience everything Zermatt has to offer, you will need to hire a mountain guide.

The difference between **guides** and **instructors** is fundamental - instructing is about 'how' and guiding is about 'where'. Ski instructors are not permitted to take you off-piste and you should not ask them to. In contrast the limiting factor with a guide is your own ability. If you are competent enough they will take you anywhere you want to go. There is no question of a guide's **ability**. Becoming one takes years and requires an intimate knowledge of everything the mountains have to offer particularly how to be safe in this notoriously unpredictable environment. Guides are not just expert skiers, first and foremost they are mountaineers: physically fit individuals, with extensive experience of mountain rescue, practice and procedure. They are also proficient rock and ice climbers and are competent and comfortable in all types of conditions. During the course of qualifying, they are tested on a wide assortment of skills including alpine technique, avalanche rescue and first aid, to name but a few. The very definition of a safe pair of hands.

Zermatt's Mountain Guide Association is one of the oldest in the Alps - it was founded over 100 years ago, in 1894. It is an extremely professional establishment that is justifiably proud of its ethos and traditions. And its individuals have played a special role in the resort's history - by the church you will find a cemetery of all *bergführer* who lost their lives whilst working in the mountains. Zermatt's guides are recognised as some of the best in the world, with a reputation that competes with the Chamoniards, just down the haute route. Most guides work independently or can be booked through the Association, which has a reservations desk on the first floor on the Alpin Center on Bahnhofstrasse (t 027 966 2460, i zermatt.ch/alpincenter, Mondays-Sundays 4pm-7pm). You need to book ahead, particularly during the spring, when their services are most in demand - don't expect to be able to hire a guide on the day you want one, particularly if you have a specific individual in mind.

And **what's on offer**? Anything you can think of - an impressive list including off-piste skiing, group ski tours (for 1 day or more), indoor and outdoor rock-climbing, ice climbing, heli-skiing, snowshoe tours, an adventure trail through the Gorner gorge. All of these activities are organised on a group basis and can be booked through the Alpin Center. You can also hire a guide

lessons & guiding

privately for any of these activities, which ensures that the route and pace suit your own ability. Packages are also available, not least for haute route tours including the classic route from Chamonix-Zermatt (→ ski touring). They will also show you around the pistes - but don't expect them to be too excited about doing it.

prices for the different activities on offer vary - and include the necessary equipment and the guide's fee. The price for a day's off-piste guiding for up to 5 people costs around CHF500 (the bigger your group, the less you pay individually) - but you are better off spending the money and coming back alive. Guides can only be booked for a whole day, and you need to have mountain rescue **insurance** to go with one of them.

If you decide to hire a guide, don't underestimate how fit you need to be to get the most out of the experience. Whilst the guide will cater the day to the standard of the least able skier in the group, he may still lead you along some tiring traverses or climbs to reach the best snow.

snapshot

best of british
The Ski Club of Great Britain was established over 100 years ago and has 'reps' in 44 major ski areas worldwide. Zermatt is one of its flagship resorts and the Club has based 2 reps in the resort for a number of years. While a rep has a number of responsibilities, such as the collection of data for snow reports, the main benefit of one to a club member is the in-resort ski orientation programme. While other tour operators have problems convincing resorts to allow its workers to show clients around the ski area, Ski Club reps are permitted to run a 6-day weekly programme. The majority of the programme is on-piste, different days for different standards of skiing, though for a lot of members the highlight of the week is the off-piste day that the Club organises, particularly true in Zermatt where the off-piste terrain is unfriendly without the right knowledge. The Club organises the guide - its contacts within Zermatt's guiding community ensure that you get an English-speaking guide - and they also sort out all the necessary equipment for you. Zermatt's Ski Club rep can be found at the hotel Sonne, Sundays 7pm-8pm, Mondays-Thursdays 6:30pm-7:30pm with an après ski party from 6:30pm on Tuesdays.

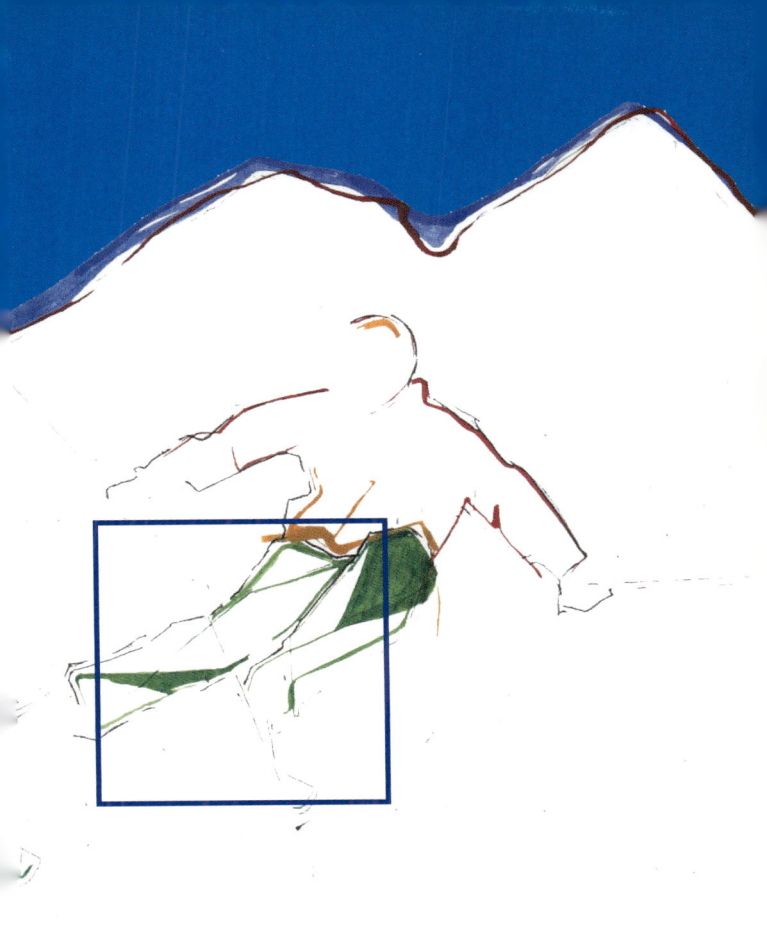

the skiing

overview

As you would expect from a resort of such infamy, the skiing isn't bad either - 400kms (in the combined Zermatt-Cervinia area) of blues, reds and blacks in a landscape of unforgettable scenery. Just don't go expecting to ski the Matterhorn. Though it is as ubiquitous as Toblerone, and the ski area has recently been renamed the "Matterhorn ski paradise" you can't actually ski on it. You can ski underneath it, alongside it, with it directly in view, but never actually on it. For amateur geologists, Zermatt's peaks are some of the best examples of Africa meeting Europe. The ridges and valleys formed due to the collision of the 2 tectonic plates millions of years ago and the divisions can be clearly seen in the rocks - if you know what you're looking for. While some of the rocks may be African, the maintenance of the pistes is most definitely Swiss - well groomed and well ordered to the extent that certain points on the mountain are designated for particular types of skiing. Signs (on the official piste map and on the mountain) indicate where there are lines of moguls (*buckelpisten*) and where the terrain is suitable for carving and freeriding. The mountain restaurants are as much of a highlight as the skiing. Such is the popularity of some - particularly in the food Mecca of Findeln (on the Rothorn) - that reservations are essential. You will wish that your stomach could be as bottomless as some of the nearby crevasses.

snapshot

vital statistics
400km of pistes (Zermatt/Cervinia) - 20% blues, 52% reds & 28% blacks
62 lifts - 9 cable cars, 18 chairs, 26 drags, 16 gondolas, 1 rack railway & 2 funiculars
off-piste - 15 itinerary routes & vast unpisted backcountry
highest point - 3820m
longest run - 22km

pistes

Each area has a fair range of pistes - easy cruisey blues, testing but doable reds and challenging blacks. While the quantity and quality of the pistes isn't in doubt, the connection between the 3 main areas is - they are badly linked by piste and by lift. As getting between them is presently a slow and somewhat frustrating process it is best to choose your area at the start of the day so you don't spend too much time on lifts. To help you get your bearings on the mountain all of the pistes are numbered and named (though the official piste map only shows the numbers). To help you further the edges of the pistes are marked by poles: on the left by a pole the colour of the piste with a small orange strip at the top and on the right by a half orange, half piste colour pole. The piste system adopts the same colour-coding used in all European resorts (➙ 'pistes' in the glossary) but it should only be used as a general guide. Although the gradient or width of each

overview

individual piste stays the same, other features such as snow conditions can change daily. A blue piste can become more testing than a nearby red, because it is over-crowded with skiers of ranging abilities or because of poor or icy conditions. And personal feelings about pistes vary greatly - an easy blue to one skier can seem like a vertical drop to another.

off-piste

In this guide we distinguish between the recognised and mapped itinerary routes and the rest of the off-piste found away from the lifts. Itinerary routes are identified by the colour yellow (on maps and the mountain) and though they are not groomed or checked at the end of the day, the resort classifies them as being "marked and protected from danger of high-altitude terrain". They will be closed if conditions are unsuitable - and for your own safety you should respect the signs.

lifts

The resort has invested in the lift system over the last few years, replacing older links with new, faster lifts - some are so luxurious that they have heated seats. And in keeping with the modernisation you will find (American-style) courtesy boxes of tissues at the bottom of some. There is a planned programme for further development until 2009, which will partly address the poor linkage between the 3 areas. The lifts used for the winter ski season are open by early December and run until the middle/end of April. The exact date changes yearly and if the snow conditions are good, the lift may open or close earlier than advertised. Opening and closing times are noted at the bottom of each lift. Information on the status of the pistes and lifts is shown on Zermatt's very own television channel, which is displayed on screens in main lift stations, the more modern cable cars and through most hotel televisions.

the areas

For the purpose of the maps and information in this guide, the ski area is divided into 6 parts - the Klein Matterhorn ski area is shown on 2 maps as are the pistes above Cervinia:
zermatt
rothorn (map a)
gornergrat (map b)
lower klein matterhorn (map c)
upper klein matterhorn (map d)
cervinia
plan maison (map e)
cime bianche (map f)
In this chapter you'll find a description of how to get to and from the slopes, the general characteristics and aspect of the area, and detail of the pistes, the off-piste and the mountain restaurants. At the back there is a more detailed table of lift information and a ski map for each area (in which the piste colours correspond to those used by the resort).

overview

coming & going
Where you start depends upon where you want to ski. With 3 valley-floor lift stations you can take your pick as to how you get up the mountain. As all the lifts from the valley-floor lift stations are 2-directional, you can also get home to them by lift.

beginners
Bluntly put, Zermatt is not the resort for those new to the sport. There are no beginners' areas close to the town - what easy slopes there are lie at least a lift ride up the mountain. And the ski back to the resort from each is beyond the ability of even the most gung-ho beginners. Of the 3 areas, the Klein Matterhorn offers the most with the greatest number of blue (so wider and gentler) pistes - the 2 ski schools hold most of their beginners' lessons up here. Even then the way home is black and steep - so beginners have to return by lift, which somewhat poops the party. The same is true for the Gornergrat and the Rothorn - although the descent from each is blue, from the latter it is a narrow path prone to unpredictable conditions and from the former the blue is red-hued in parts. Perhaps the resort is aware of its limitations, as it does not sell a beginners lift pass.

intermediates
As over 100kms of Zermatt's 194kms of pistes are red, intermediates will find something to suit their level - each of the areas above Zermatt have their fair share. The same is true over in Cervinia - so much so that one wonders if there was a glut of red paint when it came to deciding the grading of the pistes. For those who like to get miles for their money the reds count among their number some of the longest you'll find in Europe. For more quantity than quality it is possible to ski all 3 of the ski areas directly above Zermatt in 1 day - but only by spending time on several lifts. And if you are keen to extend your technique to other disciplines, the designated areas for moguls and carving let you dip your toe into the water.

experts
The statistics for the resort show that there are over 70kms of black pistes in the Zermatt ski area. But with the exception of the black underneath the Patrullarve chair on the Rothorn, the rest are a motley collection of narrow descents, which are probably graded black because the conditions on them are generally undesirable. Experts should look instead to the itinerary routes - 15 in total - the area at the top of Rote Nase and Stockhorn on the Gornergrat being particularly littered with yellow poles. But you can only ski there after January, as these routes don't open until then (when the snow is likely to be better). Other options include the Chamois and Marmotte routes on the Rothorn, which need decent coverage before being

overview

attempted, and routes 13 & 14 on the Klein Matterhorn, which conversely need stable snow conditions to be open.

boarders

Those on one plank instead of two should enjoy the sweeping runs as much as their duo-equipped companions but may find getting home a frustrating activity - whichever area you choose, the final descent to the village will not score high on the enjoyment scale. The paths from both the Rothorn and the Gornergrat areas are flat and narrow. The descent from the Klein Matterhorn has a slightly more favourable gradient, but one which flattens out for the last 100 metres.

Officially Zermatt has 2 snowparks. The real thing is the Gravity Park (i bergbahnen.zermatt.ch) on the Klein Matterhorn. There is also a smaller and less frequented park on the Gornergrat, just below the Rotenboden train station.

summer skiing

The pistes above Trockener Steg on the Klein Matterhorn are open during the summer and autumn months. It's not a huge area, but it's something different from the usual summer beach holiday.

non-skiers

With 30 km of winter hiking paths the resort recognises that not all of its winter visitors come to ski - the number of winter walkers almost equals the number of skiers, and the resort caters for them well. It is possible to pay for one-way or return trips on the gondolas and cable cars and some chairlifts. A winter walking lift pass is available (the Peak Pass ➜ lift passes), and the resort produces a comprehensive pamphlet - winterwanderen - describing the various *'wanderwegs'* and snowshoe trails. The leaflet explains when the routes will be open after a snowfall, their difficulty and length (ranging from 2 to 5kms and taking as little as 45 minutes to 2 hours) - and you can find yourself rambling through beautiful snow-covered pine forests or over rocky outcrops amid the mountain peaks. For a longer ramble, you can combine different routes. The routes are also marked in less detail on the resort's official piste maps, or alternatively OS maps can be bought from the bookshops in the village.

The range of other activities for non-skiers, both on and off the snow, is also extensive (➜ events & activities).

rothorn

The Rothorn is the most northern of the ski areas directly above Zermatt with a west-facing aspect and a view to the Matterhorn and the inhospitable slopes (to skiers) on the other side of the village. Zermatt's first ski lift was constructed here in 1942 and linked the village to the sunny slopes of Sunnegga (now the name of the first mid-station). In the late 1970s the original lift was consigned to memory and replaced by the Sunnegga funicular (a cog-and-pinion railway and the first of its kind in Switzerland) - this lift still moves the masses up the mountain today. The skiing on the Rothorn is extremely pleasant - a full compliment of pistes, which will please any level of skier. Beginners will find enough blues that aren't overly challenging, the reds are fun and will test intermediates and the 4 itinerary routes keep the more advanced skiers happy. If you want to iron out your mogul technique this is a good place to head - there are a number of deliberately bumpy areas - from a short, shallow section to the right of the piste at the top of the Rothorn to a steeper, more testing section on the way down to Gant. The mountain restaurants also add to the overall feeling of pleasantness - ski here when you want to prioritise a work-out for your stomach above a work-out for your legs. The Rothorn is home to the small hamlet of Findeln, which is known for its abundance of excellent places to dine - and confirmed by the fact that the

map a

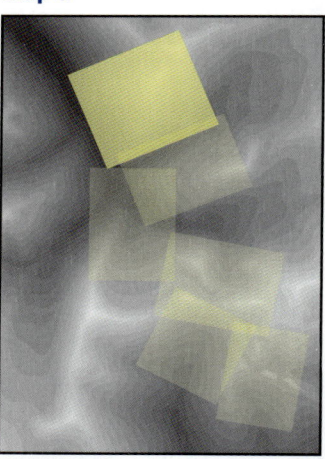

snapshot

out of interest
highest point - 3103m
aspect - w
access - underground funicular
lifts - 1 underground funicular, 1 cable car, 3 chairs & 2 gondolas
pistes - long blues, varied reds, 1 bumpy & 1 smooth black
off-piste - 4 itinerary routes
restaurants - 13

highlights & hotspots
food, glorious food
the rothorn rock collection
chamois spotting
patchy snow on the home run

rothorn

reach. At the top you can ski down to Gant, the crossroads of the Rothorn and Gornergrat areas.

pistes

The **blues** of note start at Blauherd. The right one runs across the width of the mountain past the Tuftern hut and the Patrullarve chairlift all the way home. True to its hue it is gentle and unchallenging - though the bottom section is a narrow track, often subject to poor conditions.

restaurants are better sign-posted than the route there. Non-skiers happy to work up an appetite first can also join in the feast - Findeln can be reached on foot from the village by a pleasant and easy stroll (about 30 minutes) up through the pine forest. They can then get home by lift (the Findeln chairlift and the Sunnegga funicular) if the increase in the girth doesn't leave a guilty conscience.

access

The starting point is the Sunnegga funicular. An easy journey that runs like clockwork, trains shoot up the mountain to Sunnegga every 10 minutes. From here you can ski down to the village or to Findeln, if your stomach is already rumbling. The Sunnegga-Blauherd gondola takes you higher to Blauherd (the next mid-station) from where you can keep going up to the top of the Rothorn (by the Blauherd-Rothorn cable car) and the highest point you can

The **reds** are enjoyable for intermediates but probably won't excite experts too much. At the top of Rothorn a left turning takes you along a red route heading north - though the main highlight is the view down the Vispa valley rather than the skiing. The piste is little more than a glorified path, probably graded red only due to its narrowness. A turn to the right takes you down a more interesting (but consequently more busy) red, which sweeps down the mountain past the Fluhalp restaurant to Gant. The status of the red from just below Blauherd (to Findeln) poses a question - on the official piste map it is marked as a red piste, but on the mountain it is lined with yellow poles (the colour used to signify an itinerary route) and the conditions at the top generally justify them.

Only 2 **blacks** to speak of. The longer starts just below Blauherd and passes

rothorn

through the forest to the bottom of the Patrullarve chair and beyond to join the blue path running back down to the village - steep in parts, it is a satisfying descent that won't leave you too short of breath. The other black is shorter but not so sweet - more often than not it is pockmarked with moguls - though the bumps tend to be large blocks of unappealing ice rather than skiable mounds, making it a relief to join the blue piste at the bottom of it.

off-piste

Of the 4 **itinerary routes** on the Rothorn, the longer and more testing descents are those known as Chamois and Marmotte, which start just below Rothorn. Running over rocky terrain, which needs a lot of snow to be completely covered, you may wish for the rock-hopping powers of their namesakes - and even then you can find yourself unceremoniously dumped in the snow when your skis hit a hidden stone. There is a shorter route at the far north end of the area - down a shallow-sided valley as far away from the tamed nature of the pistes as you can get in this area - you may be lucky enough to stumble across some wildlife.

The off-piste proper is limited, but there is some scope for powder bashing just beyond the piste markers, most noticeably down the red to Gant and parallel to the black run underneath the Patrullarve chairlift.

eating & drinking

It's difficult to go wrong in this area, especially if you head to the small cluster of buildings known as Findeln. Reached by the blue path from the top of the Eisflush chairlift, the piste through the hamlet is lined with signs to restaurants. An alternative way to get there is along the is-it-a-red-is-it-an-itinerary descent from just below Blauherd. All of Findeln's restaurants have terraces overlooking the slopes and forests of the Gornergrat ski area. Oh, and the Matterhorn.

The first restaurant you pass as you ski down to Findeln is **paradies** (t 027 967 3451). The smallest of the bunch, it is the hardest to find despite the signs from the piste - as it is hidden among (and cunningly disguised as one of) Findeln's numerous stadels, which sadly for its owners means that many keep on going.

Next along the descent is the slope-side **chez vrony** (t 027 967 2552), one of the few mountain restaurants known outside the resort. The celebrity choice, specialities include excellent rösti - with toppings such as traditional egg and ham, or the more exotic duck livers - and a bewildering range of alcoholic coffees. And in Vrony's idyllic setting it's hard not to indulge - particularly if you can position yourself on one of the beautifully carved wooden chairs lining the expansive ground floor terrace, complete with cuddly cushions and

rothorn

blankets. Inside there are 3 levels - the first and second floors each have a small balcony. Overall, Vrony's feels a more commercial operation than some of the other restaurants nearby - despite the 200 person capacity it's best to book, particularly if you have a particular table in mind. No credit cards are accepted, but if you find yourself short of cash, you can arrange to pay your bill down in town later on. Vrony also opens on Wednesday evenings, if more than 20 people book - fun for a big group.

There are 3 more restaurants below Vrony. Of these **adlerhütte** (t 027 967 1058) is the runt of the litter. Anywhere else it would be the gastro star and the fare is still superior to that served in restaurants elsewhere on the mountain - here it suffers the misfortune of being in the right place at the wrong time.

enzian (t 027 967 6404), named after a small blue flower seen in the summertime, is a cute little place to stop for a bite to eat or a particularly good glühwein. Situated at the top of some steps behind the small chapel of St. James, the inside is small and extremely cosy. Decorated throughout with alpine curios, there is actually more seating on the benches on the terrace than in the rustic interior. No credit cards accepted.

findlerhof (t 027 967 2588), or Franz and Heidi's to the regulars, is viewed by many as Vrony's main competitor. Smaller and more homely, its Matterhorn view and food are just as spectacular. Located at the bottom of a steep path, it is about 150m from the piste, and just below the chapel of St. James and Enzian. Service is very friendly and the wine list very decent - though bear in mind the walk back to the piste as you order a second bottle.

Away from Findeln the **fluhalp** (t 027 967 2597) on the red piste from the Rothorn down to Gant offers the best unimpeded view of the Matterhorn and the best gourmet alternative.

The **tuftern** hut on the other side of the mountain is not so gourmet nor as pricey. Small and sparsely furnished, it is run by 2 brothers who become friendlier the more German you speak (no matter how badly). Here the drinks menu is significantly longer than the food menu, and what little food is available is simple - soup served from a tureen, hunks of cheese or sausage served with bread, and good tarts. But with the woodburner in the dining area that is enough to take the bite out of any frosting. Also it is by far the cheapest option on this hill and being at the end of one of the official walking trails, it's a good place for skiers to meet non.

There is also a restaurant at each of the mid-stations. The **rothorn** (t 027 967 2675) at the top of the Blauherd-Rothorn cable car is the highest food-

rothorn

hall. Just beside it is the **edelweiss** (t 027 967 2236), an outdoor bar, open only in good weather.

The **blauherd** (t 027 967 3524) at Blauherd is the largest restaurant on the Rothorn. An over-priced self-service outfit, it doesn't need to worry because its convenient location is enough to ensure some clientele - just as long as they remain ignorant to the culinary delights elsewhere. Outside you'll find the sometimes aptly named **sunshine bar**.

The best use of the **sunnegga** restaurant (t 027 967 3046) is as a meeting point - it is beside the top of the Sunnegga funicular, and the Findeln chairlift and the main piste from Blauherd runs past it. Otherwise, it's a large, functional partly table-, partly self-service place dishing up slightly better food than some of its contemporaries on the mountain.

Though you can après in any of the Findeln restaurants (as long as you keep an eye on the time of the last lift), any of the 3 restaurants on the route home to Zermatt is as suitable - and all of them also serve lunch. The first you reach is **othmar's skihütte** (t 027 967 1761) below the bottom of the Patrullarve chair (it can also be reached from the black piste). It has a deceptively rustic appearance, despite its relative youth (not yet 50 years old), but the vibe is youthful despite the deception. Next is **ried** (t 027 967 4284), the most subdued of the 3 options - suitable for a more chilled out warming glass of glühwein. And you may need such a restorative drink for the **olympia stübli** (t 027 967 2407), the last option and the most bustling après spot, where you can enjoy the live music from its 2 terraces. It is also open in the evening for dinner or drinks, if you can face the uphill walk from the village.

bad weather

An advantage of the Sunnegga funicular is that it is not affected by adverse weather. Though it only takes you to the Sunnegga mid-station, at least it means the very keen can get on the mountain and stop annoying the rest.

getting home

All of the upper pistes converge just above the Patrullarve chairlift. From here you can get home **on skis** on a blue-but-narrow path or a steep-but-wide black (the black joins the blue lower down). Then you can ski to just above the Sunnegga lift station or carry on along the path past the Grand Hotel Schönegg (➔ hotels) as far as the snowline goes. Take extra care from the Grand Hotel as you are skiing on a road and may encounter an electric car, who will most definitely win. There are 3 points on the hill where you can decide to give your legs a rest and return home **by lift** - at the top of Rothorn, at Blauherd or at Sunnegga.

gornergrat

The Gornergrat is as much of a destination for non-skiers as it is for skiers - the only way up from the village is by train, a scenic ride enjoyable for those without a tight agenda (sit on the right side for the best view of the Matterhorn). Skiers with more urgency to get on the slopes will definitely get fidgety - the train's languid 40 minute journey (with an average uphill speed of 28km/h) can seem like an eternity. As the skiing on the Gornergrat can be reached from the top of the Rothorn (after the 3 lifts to the top, a ski down the red piste to Gant and then another lift) they may prefer to go that way. But for over-excited early risers the train offers a rare opportunity to get on the slopes before most skiers have turned off their alarm - the first train leaves at 8am. The GGB Gornergrat-Monte Rosa-Bahnen company (t 027 921 4111, i ggb.ch) is responsible for running the train line and also organises a number of activities during the winter months, such as moonlit and torchlit skiing (➥ events & activities).

Like the Rothorn, the Gornergrat has similar views of that rock and a number of west facing slopes. The Stockhorn area has a more northerly aspect, which keeps the snow powdery for longer. This is the area for thrill-seekers as it is home to the infamous Triftji bumps (only open from the beginning of February). More leisurely skiers will enjoy the pistes below the Gornergrat lift station down past Riffelberg and

map b

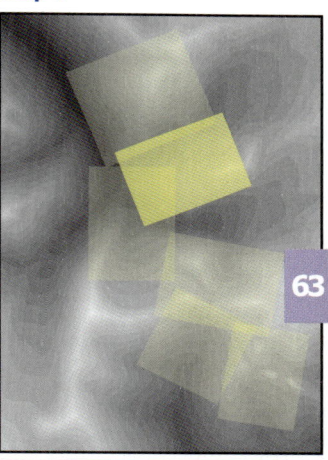

63

snapshot

out of interest
highest point - 3405m
aspect - nw, w & sw
access - mountain railway
lifts - 1 mountain railway, 4 cable cars & 5 chairs
pistes - wide & gentle blues, long & steep reds
off-piste - 5 itinerary routes
restaurants - 10

highlights & hotspots
an epic train ride
glaciers as far as the eye can see
the triftji bumps

gornergrat

Riffelalp to Winkelmatten - an altogether smoother descent. While skiers will find plenty to keep them amused, non-skiers are also well provided for. At the top of the train line (3100m), they can enjoy the view from the terrace of the Kulm hotel, Europe's highest, or get the blood pumping by donning snowshoes (for hire at the Riffelalp (2210m), Riffelberg (2582m) and Rotenboden (2819m) stations) - toboggans are also available. If conditions are friendly a further ascent up the mountain can be made from the Gornergrat to Hohtälli and then the Rote Nase peak, sandwiched between the Gorner and Findel glaciers, and offering a spectacular view. For statistics collectors, the railway on the Gornergrat is Europe's highest cogwheel railway and the Riffelalp resort (2222m) (➞ hotels) has Europe's highest outdoor pool - though to deter the foolhardy this is not open in the winter months.

access

Trains leave from the Gornergrat station (opposite the Bahnhof) every 25 minutes or so for most of the day (8am-4:30pm), and then less frequently until just before 10pm (an additional lift pass is needed for the evening trains). The train splits along the route - the front half travelling without stopping to the Gornergrat peak, whilst the back half stops at the small stations of Rotenboden, Riffelalp, Riffelboden, Riffelberg and Findelbach (1770m).

Timetables for the train are dotted around the mountain at various points: such as at the entrance to the Riffelalp resort. You can get to the Gornergrat pistes from the Rothorn area - from Gant, up the Gant-Hohtälli cable car - but the most direct route is on the train.

pistes

The main **blue** piste begins at the top of the Gornergrat and passes all the way to Winkelmatten. Along the way it splits into 3 (before merging again at Riffelberg) giving some variety, all 3 branches are true blue.

Of the 3 **reds**, 2 out of the 3 aren't bad - long and fun, but not too difficult for strong intermediates. The third, from Hohtälli (known as White Hare) is narrow and steep at the top giving it a tricky start.

No **blacks** to speak of, but with so many itinerary routes, who's counting?

gornergrat

off-piste

Until recently the **itinerary routes** in the Triftji area were classified as black or red runs. Now the area is left ungroomed with 5 recognised routes down the open bowl. Mogul seekers (and orthopaedic surgeons) will delight in the knee-jolting terrain and, because the slopes face north and are at a high altitude, the snow is generally good. Though the area is not opened until the beginning of February (as the rocky terrain underneath needs decent snow coverage before it is skiable), it normally stays open until May. One route takes you down to Gant from where you can return to the skiing on the Gornergrat or go up to Blauherd on the Rothorn. Another leads to Findeln - though you can't return to the Gornergrat from here as there is only one lift (the Findeln chairlift) which links to Sunnegga on the Rothorn. The latter part of this route is narrow and often mogulled, but makes for a pretty descent through the trees.

eating & drinking

Not a patch on the epicurean delights of Findeln, but there are enough choices to keep your stomach from making too many noises.

The **bärghüs grünsee** (t 027 967 2553) is a large restaurant, with a large terrace to take advantage of its south-facing aspect, its view of the Matterhorn and the tree-lined valley down to Findeln, and its vantage spot for skier-watching - experts from Triftji and the less expert from the more sedate reds. The inside feels cosy but is able to accommodate large groups. All the food is home-made, with the usual choices, including a wider than normal range of soups and an excellent *assiette valaisanne*.

The huge self-service **riffelberg** (t 027 966 6500) restaurant provides standard food seemingly geared to the families using the nearby children's area. The attached conservatory is an option for après - happy hour (or happy half) runs 4pm-4:30pm every day, when you can get 2 drinks for the price of 1. Slightly lower down you will find the imposing **riffelberg hotel**.

The main restaurant at the Riffelalp Resort is the **alexandre** (in the hotel), which offers a daily buffet of local produce at lunch-times - on sunny days, you can enjoy this outside on the hotel's large terrace. The **pavillon** just opposite only opens on good weather days because it only has seating outside. The highlight here are the huge and very tasty Matterhorn shaped pizzas - ignore the gimmick, they're delicious.

The **alphitta** (t 027 967 2114), below the Riffelalp resort is just another of the charming alpine restaurants that Zermatt does so well. This sounds patronising, but isn't intended to be as the Alphitta is exactly that - another of

gornergrat

the charming alpine restaurants that Zermatt does so well. The terrace is particularly lovely and the tartan blankets they provide mean you can enjoy it even on colder days.

Just above the Gornergrat station, the **kulm hotel und restaurant gornergrat** (t 027 966 6400) sits in an imposing grey stone building topped by an observatory dome. The main reason to go is so you can say you've visited Euope's highest hotel.

The highest place for a pitstop is the **rote nase snack stop** (t 027 966 6400), which takes its name from the the nearby peak, but a *'rote nase'* may well be what you leave with if you spend too long on the terrace surrounded by the ultra reflective glaciers. Though its opening hours are somewhat sporadic, even if it's closed it's worth spending a few minutes on the terrace to take in the fantastic view - with adequate spf.

For après there are 2 options lower down (though both serve lunch as well). The livelier of the two is the **chämi-hitta** (t 027 967 1096) - and the loud music means you'll hear it before you see it. As you'd expect it is wooden inside, warmly-lit and with a Matterhorn facing terrace.

moos (t 027 967 4770) is quieter and more of a place for a *kaffee und kuchen* than a dance on the table. On the blue track from Furi to Winkelmatten, the surrounding forest just about lets through the late afternoon sun.

bad weather

Unlike train lines in the UK, snow (or leaves or anything) rarely affects the Gornergrat line.

getting home

From the Gornergrat the quickest way home **on skis** is down the blue piste past Riffelberg and Riffelalp. This splits just above Furi - left to Winkelmatten and right to Furi. If your journey home starts higher you can return along the red piste to Riffelberg - make sure you take the left turning and not right to Gant, or getting home could take longer than planned. Getting all the way home **by lift**, (and partly by train), is possible - from the top of the Stockhorn cable car to Zermatt. The pistes run parallel to the train line, so if you change your mind (in either direction) you have various get-on or get-out options.

klein matterhorn

The biggest and the highest of Zermatt's ski areas, the Klein Matterhorn is also the link to Italy. It is easy to see from the shape of its main peak (a miniature version of its big brother) how the "little Matterhorn" got its name. With a vertical drop of 2000m, the height takes your breath away... literally. There are few other places in Europe where you ski at such a high altitude. And with such a distance to travel, the ascents by cable car can be as much of an adventure as the descent - crossing deep chasms and making great vertical progress. Though there is little danger of suffering from altitude sickness, coming from ground level the air is thin enough to make you short of breath. Consequently you should take precautions - walk slowly at the very top and drink lots of fluids. Children under 3 years old are not allowed to the top because the altitude affects them more. Those with loftier ambitions can take a lift to the summit of the Klein Matterhorn. The Klein Matterhorn is also home to the longest chairlift to be built on a glacier - the Furggsattel, which starts in Switzerland and ends in Italy (though you only ski to Zermatt).

As most of the slopes face to the north, conditions in this area can be bitterly cold during the early months of the season, when the Matterhorn stands between the sun and your tan - so make sure you take enough layers. Towards the end of the season, this can

map c & d

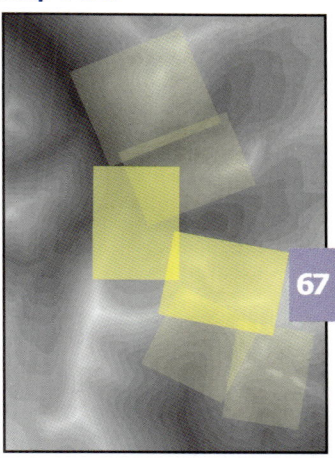

snapshot

out of interest
highest point - 3820m
aspect - nw & w
access - gondola & cable car
lifts - 4 cable cars, 2 chairs, 4 drags & 2 gondolas
pistes - wide & open blues, varied reds, narrow blacks
off-piste - 5 itinerary routes
restaurants - 17

highlights & hotspots
europe's highest cable car
iglu-dorf
zum see
itinerary routes 13 & 14

klein matterhorn

be an advantage - as any fresh snow that falls melts more slowly here than on the Gornergrat or Rothorn.

upper v lower

The skiing on the Klein Matterhorn is covered by 2 maps in this guide. One covers the section below the mid-station of Trockener Steg and includes the mid-stations known as Furgg, Furi and Schwarzsee (the '**lower klein matterhorn**'). The other covers the section from the very top down to Trockener Steg (the '**upper klein matterhorn**') - you pass through the lower Klein Matterhorn to reach this.

access

The starting point for both the upper and lower sections is the Klein Matterhorn lift station at the south end of the village. The Matterhorn Express takes you to Schwarzsee (close to the Matterhorn's sheer sides), stopping at Furi and Areloid along the way. If you want to get to the Klein Matterhorn peak get off at Furi and change onto the Furi-Trockener Steg cable car.

pistes

Those used to **blue** slopes being nearer the village will be surprised that all except one are found above Trockener Steg - the glacier's wide and gentle snowfields are ideal territory for beginners to practise their technique and for the rest to practise their speed. The only blue below Trockener Steg runs from Schwarzsee to Areloid - a short and gentle run, it is ideal for practising beginners who can take the Matterhorn Express back up and try it again.

The **reds** from the top of the Klein Matterhorn to Trockener Steg are made for speedy carving turns. The piste at the very top is a red - it starts at the end of the long rock tunnel (176m) with an initial descent over glacial fields, before dropping down the mountain, with Italy on your left and Zermatt below you to the right. At the top it is imperative to stay on the piste because of the glaciated terrain on either side. The red path to the Gandegghütte exists only to ensure that the restaurant gets some winter clientele - and for which we are all grateful though in places it is tortiously flat. 2 reds run from Schwarzsee - the White Pearl is a pleasant descent with views over the Zmutt valley - lower down it flattens

klein matterhorn

out, so make sure you get up a bit more speed to move you along. The other to Furgg is not difficult, but its narrowness and the steepish drop off on both sides can be a little off-putting.

To complete the topsy-turvy picture all the **black** runs are found below Trockener Steg. The first from Furgg to Furi is narrow, steep and often icy. As it is the most direct route home from this area, it often resembles a battlefield at the end of the day as too many skiers, most of them out of control, thrash their way down. The black from Areloid is of a similar nature, though it tends to be quieter.

summer skiing

The Klein Matterhorn glacier is open to skiers and boarders in the summer and is the biggest and highest summer snowsports area in Europe. Worth it for novelty value - the skiing isn't extensive or particularly difficult if you're an intermediate or better. The pistes (a total of 21kms) are red and blue and run between the Klein Matterhorn and Trockener Steg.

snowpark

A bona fide snowpark (known as the Gravity Park) sits between the Furggsattel chairlift and the Gandëgg draglift during the winter season. As parks go it's one of the better ones. There is usually a well-maintained halfpipe and quarterpipe, a skiercross, and separate sections for rails and kickers (with jumps of varying difficulties). During the summer the park is built beside the Plateau Rosa draglift and is open from July to November.

off-piste

With 5 **itinerary routes** the Klein Matterhorn has plenty of options on which to test your technique and your fear. Between Trockener Steg and Furgg, there are 2 wide and open ungroomed fields, which can be a powder hound's delight after a heavy snowfall. Both are testing but enjoyable enough to convince you to try routes 13 & 14 lower down... where you may curse either at your leisure or atop some extremely big moguls. Reached from Schwarzsee these routes are favourites among the skiing regulars. The extent of each is marked by a left and right pole (itinerary routes normally only have one) - and it's a good idea to stay between them. The top section of both routes is deceptively flat and wide, giving no indication of the high moguls and unforgiving conditions that often lie below. As you descend, each route becomes significantly steeper and narrower, passing down a tree-lined gully. The moguls towards the bottom can be almost unskiable, depending upon when snow last fell, and bare patches appear towards the end of the season. Both routes join the red track through the forest. The last itinerary route in this area also runs off this track

klein matterhorn

- and provides an alternative and more direct route to Zum See. It only justifies this status because it is often bare and obstacles include a road - make sure to use your green cross code.

Away from the itinerary routes, there is ample off-piste proper. But only play in it with a knowledgable guide - skiing off-piste without one is rarely a good idea and it shouldn't be considered in the Klein Matterhorn's glaciated terrain. Below the snow covered surface lurk many dangers, including invisible and potentially fatal crevasses that only a guide will know about. With a guide the choice is then yours - a particularly stunning route passes underneath the west side of the Klein Matterhorn over the Unterer Theodulgletscher (Under Theodul glacier) overlooked by the Gandegghütte - with names like that Lord of the Rings fans will wonder whether J.R.R. Tolkein ever visited the area.

eating & drinking

There is a sprinkling of eateries on the upper slopes and a veritable gathering lower down. Starting at the top the **panorama bar** is the light at the end of the long tunnel, at the top of the Trockener Steg-Klein Matterhorn cable car. Inside drinks and snacks are available, but no loo - the nearest is at the other end of the tunnel and costs you CHF1.

As the less guttural name suggests, the **testa grigia** restaurant is actually across the Italian border. Despite the rather chaotic feel inside, it is a good place for a pit-stop before the long descent to Cervinia.

The Trockener Steg mid-station has 2 restaurants in 1 - on the ground floor an eponymous self-service and the **pizza cervino** (t 027 967 1812) on the first floor. Both have a terrace and a rather souless feel compared to the family run or mountain hut choices elsewhere. Just below the mid-station is an outdoor bar aptly called the **sunshine bar**, from where you can consider the Matterhorn up close whilst nursing a restorative glühwein.

Slightly higher up is the **gandegghütte** (t 079 607 8868). Built in 1885, "le vrai Refuge du Montagne" perches on the edge of a cliff at 3030m, overlooking the Unterer Theodulgletscher with fantastic views towards both Matterhorns. A good menu and good food makes the lengthy and in places uphill traverse from the piste worthwhile. Sheepskin-lined seats and a blazing fire make it cosy and the climbing and skiing relics that line the walls make you realise that with your modern carving technology you have no excuse.

The only option at Furgg is the self-service **käsestube furgg** (t 027 967 6195). But it could be worse. The

klein matterhorn

queues that often form are its only disadvantage - with only 1 line for everything it can take some time to get what you want. Most of the seating is outside on the terrace, a sunny spot with the almost compulsory great views.

hermetje (t 027 967 7610) is a welcome stop on the sometimes gruesome black run from Areloid to Furi. Its smallish size is not a problem as it's only visited by the few skiers good enough to try the run - or by very lost, less good ones. The pasta dishes are recommended for a warming and tasty injection of carbohydrate.

At Schwarzsee the choice is between old and new. Old is the long-standing **hotel schwarzsee** (t 027 967 2263) and new is **iglu dorf** (i igludorf.com). The latter is new every year, being a bona fide igloo - worth a visit just to marvel at its construction. You can also eat, drink and sleep here - fondues at lunchtime and in the evening, with morning tea in your sleeping bag and breakfast at the hotel. After a run of snowy days, the igloo can be difficult to spot.

Lower down and at the foot of the the Matterhorn's north face is **stafelalp** (t 027 967 3062), which is normally quiet though only because of its out of the way location. You may come across some exhausted and less than fragrant skiers who have just completed the Chamonix-Zermatt haute route (➙ ski touring), which ends close by and can watch their delight at the food and drink on offer, including a particularly good apple strudel.

There is a cluster of restaurants above and below the Furi lift station including the **furi** (t 027 966 2777) **simi** (t 027 967 2695), and the **alm** (t 027 967 1646) - all serving reasonable food in varying rustic surrounds. The **pizzahütte** and **farmerhaus** sit next door to each other just below the lift station - the former couldn't be further from the English version with the same name and the latter serves an exceedingly good selection of home made cakes.

Considered by many to be the best restaurant on the mountain - if not in the Alps - **zum see** (t 027 967 2045) regularly wins awards for its cuisine and it's hard to choose from the mouth-watering menu. Housed in a old farmers hut in the tiny hamlet of the same name, it can be reached from Stafelalp or Furi. Bigger groups should try to reserve the upstairs room, which can seat about 20 (cosily). And leave room for pudding - the mille-feuille is not to be missed.

It would be a shame to limit a visit to **blatten** (t 027 967 2096) to après alone, as the food on offer is generally excellent. But being below Furi on the route home, après is why most skiers go. Housed in an old chalet on the side

klein matterhorn

of the piste, drinking (and eating) takes place inside on the ground floor or the low-ceilinged mezzanine - in the attached winter garden or on sunny days on the terrace facing the Matterhorn. The menu changes with the seasons - winter fare is more hearty with warming soups and polentas, then as it warms up the food lightens up with a spring menu of asparagus and lamb. An ideal meeting point for groups of skiers and non-skiers - it is only a 30 minute walk from the Klein Matterhorn lift station.

The other choice for après is the **hennu stall** (t 027 966 3510), where the emphasis is most definitely not on the food. The live music that plays inside during the colder months moves outside as things warm up. And if the tapping of your toes doesn't keep you warm, the fires blazing away in the wooden barrels on the terrace will. As will the assortment of tonsil-burning shots of schnapps - ask for yours to be served on the specially designed ski.

bad weather
If the weather is bad, the lifts on the Klein Matterhorn tend to be the first to close. Being the highest ski area, most of the skiing is above the tree-line so you would be lost in a referenceless sea of swirling white.

getting home
There are 3 ways to get home **on skis**: the red piste from Schwarzsee; the itinerary routes 13 and 14 (if open, and if you have enough energy); and the black from Furgg to Furi. If you are returning home late and the lift that links Furgg to Schwarzsee is closed, the black is your only option. The last section of the descent (from Furi to Zermatt) is a red piste, though towards the very end of the season you'll probably need to get home from Furi by cable car.

If you decide you want to get home **by lift**, the best place to decide is at Trockener Steg - from here it's an easy journey by cable car to Furi and then the Matterhorn Express gondola to Zermatt. Lower down the mountain, Furgg is the next option - though you have to go back up first (on the Furgg-Schwarzsee gondola) before getting on the Matterhorn Express.

breuil-cervinia

map e & f

This is a very different side of the mountain - in name and in aspect. The Matterhorn becomes Il Cervino (hence the resort's title) and presents a very different and somehow less inspiring face. The slopes face south and more often than not they bask in Italian sunshine. You'll be glad you've chosen to stay in Zermatt as you approach the resort (2000m). A monstrosity of high-rise concrete accommodation buildings, it was built at the order of Mussolini for the express purpose of skiing. But up away from all that grey, the skiing is delightful. Altogether more gentle than that in Zermatt - a mogul is an oversight on the part of the pisteurs, as smooth and sleek is the name of the game. Which does mean magnificently groomed and maintained intermediate pistes, and some of the longest vertical descents you'll find in Europe. The run down to the resort from Testa Grigia (the crossing point between Zermatt and Cervinia) is 11kms (7 miles) of cruising bliss. But this is a mere sprint compared to the 22kms of piste down to the small village of Valtournenche. And perhaps the motorway nature of the pistes explains the speeds at which the Italians ski - a bit like the way they drive.

Since most of the slopes face south you can often top up your tan as you enjoy warm spring skiing from the middle of the season onwards. It also means that the snow thaws during the day, re-freezes overnight - making it icy in the

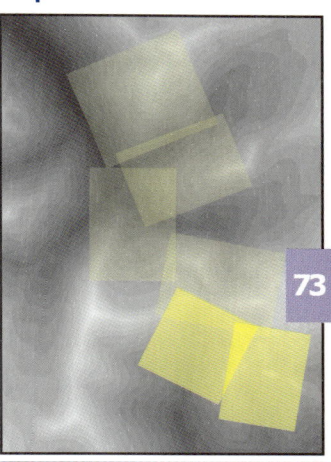

snapshot

out of interest
highest point - 3233m
aspect - s
access - gondola & cable car
lifts - cable car, chairs & gondola
pistes - cruisey blues, cruisey reds, very grey blacks
off-piste - limited
restaurants - 10

highlights & hotspots
22kms of red piste down to valtournenche
pasta & chianti for lunch
knowing you're staying in zermatt

breuil-cervinia

morning and soft in the afternoon. However, the resort has the best snow record of any in Italy (because of the closeness to so many glaciers, and the relatively high overall altitude), so this is only a problem late in the season. Nearly all of the pistes lie above the tree-line, so it's not a place to go when the visibility is poor.

If you do venture over the border, take your passport - there are customs points on the lifts back over to Zermatt. Whilst the guards rarely check, if they do and you don't have it or an identity card with you, you will not be allowed back into Switzerland and somebody will have to go to Zermatt to get it for you.

plan maison & cime bianche

Like the Klein Matterhorn, the skiing above Cervinia is covered by 2 maps in this guide. '**plan maison**' covers the skiing to the right underneath the Matterhorn and directly above the resort. '**cime bianche**' covers the skiing to the left (as you look down the mountain from Testa Grigia) to Valtournenche - the skiing here is often wonderfully quiet and great for carving. Reached by taking the left track from the red piste down from Testa Grigia, just before Bar Ventina - get some speed up beforehand, as it flattens out.

access

The easiest way to get there, if it's open, is from the top of the Klein Matterhorn (by the Trockener Steg-Klein Matterhorn cable car). From the top it's a short ski, first on a red, then on a blue (don't miss the turning on the left) with a small uphill walk to Italy at the end. The Gandegg and Testa draglifts from Trockener Steg are a longer and more tiring option by draglift - the second ends beside Testa Grigia, so there is no uphill walk into Italy - just relief that you made it.

pistes

The bulk of Cervinia's **blue** runs lie above the Plan Maison development (a shopping mall-like complex) at the top of the Breuil-Plan Maison gondola. The slopes are a maze of criss-crossing pistes, all of indeterminate nature and appeal. The blues over in Cime Bianche are similar. Skiers of all levels would enjoy any of them, though beginners staying in Zermatt may struggle to reach them, as there are a couple of stiff reds to negotiate first.

breuil-cervinia

Intermediates will get a real confidence boost by flying down them. And a bit of practise before trying the Sabato Sprint - a speed skiing run just above Plan Maison which is Cervinia's answer to Les Arcs' Kilometre Lancé.

Boarders bored with Zermatt's Gravity Park, or wanting to perfect their tan while they perfect their 360s, will find Cervinia's terrain park above the Plan Maison development.

The best runs in the area are undoubtably **red** - over half of the runs around Cervinia are categorised as such, though some skiers may disagree with the over-cautious grading. The piste from Testa Grigia is a red - you have to ski it whether you intend to ski in the Plan Maison or Cime Bianche areas. The red descent from Testa Grigia to Cervinia is wide and sweeping, perfect for carving turns. When conditions are good the 22kms run down to Valtournenche is one of the best you will find. Descending to 1520m, conditions can be variable lower down - there will be signs at the top of the Valtournenche gondola to let you know what to expect before you commit yourself. Once committed the only exit is at the bottom. Elsewhere there are plenty of other reds for intermediates to cruise without too much effort.

Cervinia's **black** runs are questionably graded - pedants would call all of them red - and all are as enthusiastically groomed as the blues and reds. The one showing the blackest tendencies runs from the top of the Cieloalto chairlift. It is not particularly steep, but is prone to iciness - often the conditions are better on the red that you eventually join.

off-piste

There are no **itinerary routes** on the official piste map and the off-piste options generally are limited - if that is what you are looking for you are better off on the other side of the border. The best of what there is is found around Cieloalto.

eating & drinking

The choice of food ranges from wood-fired pizzas to fine dining, and as local produce is used it's rare to get a bad meal. Local specialities include smoked ham, polenta, and meat stew and you can find plenty of good, fresh pasta. Local ways to wash it down include genepi and grappa - if you have the stomach for them. While the food (and wine) can be excellent, the other facilities can be more basic.

Restaurants will accept Swiss francs, but the exchange rate tends to be in their favour rather than yours, though as prices are significantly lower than in Zermatt you can probably forgive them the odd centime.

The **bar ventina** is the first stop on the way to the Cime Bianche area. A self-

breuil-cervinia

service place, it is big inside and out - the terrace being a particularly good sun-trap. Food ranges from hot meals to sandwiches and for reasons that are not explained, it does not serve french fries - with fierce notices to that effect on the walls!

Further down in Cime Bianche, you will find **lo baracon** an idyllic stone building beside the Roisette chairlift, **la motta (da felice)** (t 0039 339 622 2216), a modest little restaurant at the top of the drag lift of the same name and **la roisette** just above the end of the Valtournenche gondola. All make for pleasant lunchspots.

Towards Cervinia, you pass the **igloo bar**, a British-run and lively eatery that serves good basic food in large portions. At the bottom of the Lago Goillet chairlift is **pousset** (t 0039 339 694 6228), another sun-trap with a balcony bedecked with more national flags than the United Nations.

les skieurs d'antan (t 0039 016 694 0214) is French in name (the 'skiers of yesteryear'), and Italian in nature. On the sun-baked terrace, you can enjoy big bowls of pasta and delicious plates of anti-pasti. The inside is equally as nice for less clement days, and service is laid-back but pleasant.

On the Plan Maison side, the choice ranges from the functional to the divine.

There are a number of places inside the Plan Maison complex itself and just outside is the **tuktu** (t 0039 016 694 8272) self-service restaurant, which is normally as crowded and mob-like as a school canteen at lunchtime.

On the same side of the hill but at the other end of the scale you will find Cervinia's shining gastro star - the **châlet etoile** (t 0039 016 694 0220). Run by the super friendly Swedish Ulla this is a must-stop lunch spot that is without question the best place to re-fuel on this side of Il Cervnio. Tables are cosily close, but once you've tasted the food, you'll just be glad you got one. To be sure, it's best to book. The menu offers pasta, polenta and grilled meats, and the house speciality is *"braserade con raclette"*, a contraption that allows you to grill meat on the top and cheese underneath, before amalgamating them on your plate. It's not somewhere to go if you are having a day off the booze - even if you manage to avoid the tempting wine list, every diner is given a digestif, made from grappa, cointreau, Grand Marnier and forest berries and aptly known as a *"bombe"*. Service is attentive, the atmosphere ambient and the room warm and rustically charming. There is a self-service section, but if you're there you're missing the point.

Both the **cime bianche** (t 0039 016 694 9046) and the **baita cretaz** (t 0039 016 694 9914) are slope-side hotels. The former has a lovely sun

breuil-cervinia

terrace and a lovely wine list, which includes a number of Italian bouquets all of which are extremely well-priced compared to similar bottles in Zermatt. The latter serves good food which is always good value.

If you're looking for a warming drink **plan torrette** (t 0039 016 694 0947) at the bottom of the Plan Torrette chairlift serves possibly the best hot chocolate on the mountain - rich, dark and creamy - which you can enjoy on the huge south-facing terrace. Pay for your food and drink before you receive it.

The **bontadini** (t 0039 335 250312) at the bottom of the lift of the same name has a lovely 2-tiered terrace, perfect for doing a bit of last minute sunbathing before you take the lift back over to Zermatt.

Further up the hill on the Swiss-Italian border the corrugated iron building that is the **rifugio de theodul** (t 0039 016 694 9400) has better views from the inside and is the last stop for some delicious Italian pasta before you head home.

No matter how tempting the wine list or the *bon accueil* of your the host, don't be tempted to stop for après this side of Il Cervino. The last lift back to Zermatt leaves around 3:30pm and if you miss it you'll land yourself with a taxi bill as well as a bar hill - very literally one for the road.

bad weather
If the weather is bad in the Zermatt valley, the Klein Matterhorn tends to be the first area to close. So unless you have your own transport or fancy a long uphill walk you won't get to Italy.

getting home
It's crucial to make sure you don't miss the last lift. Although Zermatt and Cervinia are close as the marmotte scampers, the trip home by road takes approx. 6 hours. The way home on skis or by lift is the same - either by the trio of chairlifts to the top of the Theodulpass or the Laghi Cime Bianche-Plateau Rosà cable car to the top of Testa Grigia. Once there you have to ski at least as far as Trockener Steg on the Klein Matterhorn before you can consider letting a lift do the work.

suggested days

If you need some ideas about where to head for something specific, below is a bit of location advice.

a good lunch
Though Zermatt doesn't do bad lunches, the best to be had is at **zum see** - as you would expect from a mountain restaurant that has been voted best in the Alps. This converted farmer's hut has a following (and a menu) that top London chefs would kill for. And the choice of mouth-watering dishes leaves you with a dilemma. If you intend to while away some hours whilst perusing the menu, get a table indoors - Zum See's surrounds fall into shadow in the afternoon. And eternal optimists who turn up on the off-chance of a table will do so in vain - to say bookings are essential is understating it. On the other side of the hill, **châlet etoile** does its bit for Italy. Get there early to make the most of the menu before the closing of the lifts forces you to return to Zermatt, kicking and screaming for more.

follow the wine route
Not the name of a run or a ski tour, just another way to plan your trip round the mountain. Most of the mountain restaurants serve Swiss wines - Zermatt being in the Valais region, where just under half of all Swiss wines are produced. Maybe start the day with a glühwein (red wine blended with nutmeg, cinnamon and lemon and for some the only way to 'enjoy' the Swiss red) - one of the best is made at **enzian** in Findeln. If you're brave (and you can find it), you can always sample the indescribable taste of the Gletscher wine over lunch. And the day wouldn't be complete without a Dole Blanche (a pink wine made from Pinot Noir and Gamay grapes), best served chilled and enjoyed on a terrace whilst watching the sun dip behind the mountains - the choice of where is endless. Of course, you could always have a schnapps to kick-start the evening - the **hennustall** being more than willing to serve you a plum, pear or apricot strain... but that's just getting silly.

bad weather
Though at times the whole area can be covered in an unfriendly white blanket, often when the Klein Matterhorn is shrouded in cloud, the Rothorn and Gornergrat are in the sun. And vice versa. If so, just go wherever the

clouds are not. The lower slopes of each area are tree-lined, which give a reference point even in bad weather. The tree-lined black under the Patrullarve chairlift on the Rothorn is the best choice for experts. On the Gornergrat, the run below the Riffelalp resort is a short but viable option suitable for all, if you can be bothered with a slow train ride for a fairly short descent. The Klein Matterhorn is least likely to be open in poor visibility and bad weather, but if you can get as far as the top of the Matterhorn Express, the red piste down from Stafelalp also runs along a tree-lined route.

miles under the belt
It doesn't get much longer than the 22kms red run to Valtournenche (the equivalent of the train journey from Täsch to Zermatt and back again, twice). As the village lies in the depths of the valley, it is best to head back up the mountain for lunch to make the most of the Matterhorn's sunny side. If you want to warm up the muscles first you could always blast down the red run to Cervinia first (half the kilometrage), but to do both and have time for lunch, make an early start.

a rollercoaster ride
Life is all ups and downs, and so is a day spent trying to ski all 3 of Zermatt's ski areas. To avoid the lovely but slow trip up on the Gornergrat train, it's best to start on the slopes of the Rothorn. From the top (hold onto your hats)... down to Gant, up to Höhtalli, down to Furi, and up to the Klein Matterhorn and down, down, down all the way home. Then spend the evening nursing your muscles and working out the vertical mileage - answers on a postcard.

a bumpy ride
Moguls aren't difficult to find. With signs on the mountain to the *"buckelpiste"* you know where they are if you want them or where to avoid if you don't. The ultimate mounds are at Triftji - not for the faint hearted or those with dodgy knees.

in poor snow
With Zermatt's claim of 365 days skiing a year, poor conditions are not a regular occurrence. But if the snow gods aren't smiling, the Klein Matterhorn glacier has had years of practice keeping conditions cold and the surface snowy.

off-piste

While none of Zermatt's off-piste routes are as well known as the Chamonix's Vallée Blanche, for those in the know the resort has an established reputation for this type of skiing. The gentler side are the itinerary routes, the most famous being found in the Stockhorn area. From February onwards, skiers and boarders tussle with the bumps and natural hits. Thanks to the overall altitude of the ski area and the mainly north-facing slopes, the snow can be powdery for days after the last snowfall. Later on in the season this means exhilirating descents through spring or corn snow. They can be skied without a guide but as conditions are variable they should not be undertaken lightly.

Unlike resorts such as Verbier (which has a lot of lift accessed off-piste) much of the best of Zermatt's untamed backcountry lies far from the markers. Large and untracked fields of untouched snow are visible from the pistes and give a taster of the extensive backcountry that lies beyond. It is often steep, often isolated and in places, often scary. The scenery too is astounding, a world away from the bashed slopes between the poles. If you have not strayed out of sight of a lift or a piste before you will not believe your eyes. Descents take you over vast expenses of snow, between seracs (huge blocks of glacial ice) and over snow-bridges that span deep crevasses out of sight of civilisation. Some powder can only be reached by a long traverse or ascending a couloir. But the effort put in to get there only heightens the experience and increases the reward. For the recreational skier, it can be an unforgettable experience - and at the very least it gives you something to talk about over afternoon tea.

Not only is the ungroomed and the unmapped rough, tough and demanding on your technique, it is also high altitude glacier skiing and should not be approached without some forethought. People die every year skiing off-piste - and almost all accidents happen because of poor preparation or over-confidence. Because of the glaciated nature of what lies beneath, it is essential to employ the services of a guide to explore it further - skiing without one can put you at real risk and you should never ever ski off-piste on your own. These inviting areas often cover cliffs and rocks and deep

off-piste

crevasses (even alongside the pistes) - difficult to get out of without somebody at the top.

Not only does going with a guide allow you to enjoy the experience without worrying about the safety aspects but it adds value in other ways too. Obviously if you simply want to ski you can just follow them down the hill, but if you have any interest in your surroundings, your guide will be a mine of information. If you want to see a huge crevasse from a safe distance most guides will be more than happy to oblige. Similiarly if there is anything you are uncomfortable with, just ask. On the mountain always pay attention to your guide - crevasses can be difficult to spot and a simple bump may conceal a gaping hole.

Wearing the right clothing is essential too. In the high mountain environment, the weather can change from warm sunshine to freezing white-out in a matter of minutes. It can be as cold as -30°C, and sunshine down in town is no guarantee of good weather on the mountain. As you're unlikely to come across a handy store selling extra layers you should take a warm skiing hat, good gloves, goggles as well as sunglasses, an extra fleece - you may need none of this, but better to take it than to leave it keeping your hotel room warm. Though you might not need to pack a lunch, a few snacks (chocolate bars or something similar) and some fluid is also a good idea. Mountain restaurants aren't quite as plentiful once you get away from the groomed and the maintained.

In addition to all that you will need an avalanche transceiver, a shovel and a probe. For some off-piste skiing you will may need to take a climbing harness and a rope - your guide will advise (and probably carry the latter). If you don't know how to use the equipment (and if you don't it's as useful as a chocolate teapot) your guide will show you. And before you go, make sure your insurance covers your adventure.

ski touring

Ever wondered about the seemingly mad bunch of skiers who walk up pistes as well as down? To the uninitiated it can seem a desparate bid to save on the lift pass, or complete disregard for a perfectly good lift system. This 'sport' is known as ski touring or ski mountaineering - the latter is perhaps a more appropriate name, given the climbing up as well as the skiing down and on a 'tour' you travel from 'a' to 'b' in the same way as hiking up mountains in summer. Ski touring means you can get to places not accessed by lift and into off-piste territory otherwise hidden from view. And believe it or not there is immense satisfaction after a physically demanding ascent or descent as well as the enjoyment of being amidst the alpine scenery, away from the mêlée of the pistes.

Obviously, different equipment is necessary. To climb up slopes you need skis with touring bindings, which unlock to allow the heel to come away from the ski as you step upwards. You also carry 'skins' - now artificial but so called because they were originally seal skins - to attach to the base of the skis during a climb to prevent them from slipping down. The precautions and preparation for off-piste skiing apply equally to touring. And doubly so, if you are planning to stay on the mountain overnight - you will be very far from your nearest Migros, so make sure you have ample provisions. And sufficient clothing - it's hard to get warm once you're cold. This is just one of the reasons to go with a backpack - though if you've never skied with one before you should be aware that it significantly changes your centre of gravity and so until you get used to it you may find your balance is a little off. Also, inform someone of your itinerary and likely time of return.

Zermatt is the launch point for numerous ski-tours, including the original *haute route* (high level road). It is an excellent place to try this type of skiing for the first time, as a number of day tours (with ascents ranging from 1-3 hours) are viable. These can be booked through the Alpin Center (➥ lessons & guiding) from late December until the middle of May - either as part of an organised group or privately. Groups normally consist of between 3 to 7 people. A tour up the Schwarztor is a good opener - a 1-hour

ski touring

climb before a descent down a glacier, while the twin peaks of Castor and Pollux offer a more challenging ascent. Ski touring is possible throughout the whole season, but March and April are when it comes into its own, as the weather is more predictable and the days are longer. And though the season officially ends in April as tourers don't need lifts, they can still enjoy what remains of the snow in May.

the haute route

Zermatt is the end of probably the best known touring route - or the beginning if you want to try it backwards. This haute route was first skied in the early 20th Century and though many other haute routes have since been established, this is considered to be the original and is now known as the Classic. If you have any yearning for this type of skiing, this route is the equivalent of a mountaineer's Everest. The route runs between Chamonix and Zermatt. It takes 6 days to complete, crosses more than 20 glaciers and totals some 10,000m of combined ascent and descent. The majority of skiers travel it from west to east, starting in Chamonix, not least because travelling to Zermatt is considered to be less tiring (with more down than up) with more stunning views - and it is hard to beat the finish under the north face of the Matterhorn. The last day brings you down into the Zmutt valley, with the first sign of civilisation being the Stafelalp mountain restaurant (serving perhaps the most welcome beer in the Alps) before an easy schuss along the scenic red piste to Furi and Zermatt.

The nights are spent in refuge huts - small buildings dotted around the mountain which provide evening meals, basic sleeping space and an escape from cold and inclement weather. The facilities aren't the height of luxury, but you should be too exhilirated (or exhausted) to mind. And you've just seen some of the most beautiful mountain scenery in the world from Mont Blanc to the Matterhorn.

As with day tours, haute route tours can be booked through the Alpin Center. For a full description of the route see Peter Cliff's book The Haute Route, published by Cordee and available from most bookstores in Zermatt.

events & activities

A king of a ski resort but a minnow on the events calendar, Zermatt doesn't see too many high profile competitions, but there are a few for those finding their competitive edge.

The first event of the winter season is the International FIS Races **mens giant slalom**, held every year in December on the Klein Matterhorn. As close as you'll get to Ski Sunday speeds, and an opportunity to buy a cow bell. Youngsters also get a look in at the **migros grand prix ski race** - a qualifying race for the biggest ski-race in Europe for children and young people aged 8 to 15 years.

Zermatt is host to Switzerland's second-biggest open-air curling tournament - the **zermatt horu trophy** - held in January every year.

All-comers can also have a go in the **night ski-touring race** held on the Rothorn every year. Those with both knees in tact can enter the **triftji bump bash** (i bumpbash.com) a 3 day competition held every year in April. This is a mogul race for amateurs and pros down the moguls in the area of the same name. And once you've bashed down the bumps you can bump away at the bash in town.

The **patrouille des glaciers** (i pdg.ch) is an extraordinary glacier patrol race held every 2 years at the end of April. There are 2 categories - 1 of which runs

snapshot

eat drink & be on skis
Described as "the most notorious restaurant race in the Alps" the Luttman/Johnson challenge was created by the imagination of Colonel Hugh Luttman-Johnson. Since the 1970s the race has been organised by the Ski Club of Great Britain. The rules seem complicated and even Einstein might struggle with the formula used - $C=(R+A) \times (M-L)/R$ Simply put, the basic aim is to visit a number of pre-selected restaurants around the ski area, spending as much time in each as possible and so skiing between them as fast as possible. Skiers race in teams of two, in either the Race (for speedsters) or the Trail (for the more leisurely) and choose their own route between the designated eating and drinking spots. Fancy dress is optional, prizes plentiful and fun inevitable.

from Zermatt to Verbier, while the other runs from Arolla to Verbier. As the name suggests it crosses over numerous glaciers, so competitors must be super-fit and excellent skiers and also competent at crevasse rescue - only for all mountain men and women.

Further information on all these events and details of more local events run for visitors to the resort are available from the tourist office or their online events calendar.

events & activities

If you need a break from the downhill grind, there are plenty of other things to keep you entertained on the snow.

Zermatt is the centre of **heliskiing** in Switzerland, with 4 permitted landing sites within easy reach (the Äschihorn-Rothorn glacier, Monte Rosa-Grenszattel, Alphubeljoch and the Theodul glacier). Trips can be organised through the Mountain Guides' association at the Alpin Center and are priced according to the number of drops you make.

For those who'd rather get around in a seated position, there are 2 main **sledging** runs. The longest is from Furi, along a path through the forest, to the top end of Winkelmatten. There is also a run on the Gornergrat from Rotenboden to Riffelberg, which takes about 10 minutes. Toboggans can be hired at the Riffelberg station, 8:30am-4pm. Day and half-day tickets are available for the train ride from Zermatt to Rotenboden, unlimited sledging between Riffelberg and Rotenboden and the return trip to Zermatt (this is free for children aged 9 years and under). Both routes are marked on the official piste map and on the map in the winter walks leaflet. If you like the idea of seeing stars (of a celestial kind), **night-time sledging** is also possible most weeknights from the beginning of January to the end of March at some point on the mountain - often with a meal thrown in for good measure (book at the Alpin Center or the Gornergrat train station). Organised **moonlit skiing** takes place once every month on the Gornergrat, with a fondue at the Kulm hotel (again book at the Gornergrat train station). As the moon only illuminates the slopes so infrequently, **torch-lit descents** are organised 3 or 4 times a month in January, February and March.

With less than 10kms of trails close to the resort (from Furi to Zermatt), Zermatt wouldn't be the first choice for lovers of **cross-country skiing** (schweigmetten). But 10kms is enough if you just want to have a go - and the SSS run lessons (→ lessons & guiding). If you get dizzy from going round and round, there are a further 20kms or so of trails lower down the valley around Täsch and Randa.

There are 6 marked **snowshoe** trails (3 on the Gornergrat and 3 on the Klein Matterhorn, including "white magic", "discovery" and "challenge") - all detailed on the winter walks leaflet map so you don't need to take a guide. The Alpin Center also has more detailed maps and full itineraries of the routes - they range in length (2kms-6½kms) and take 1-3½ hours. To go off-trail, book a guide from the Alpin Center (→ lessons & guiding). Snow shoes can be rented from most of the major sports stores in the town. On Wednesday evenings you can strap tennis rackets to your soles for a night-time snowshoe with dinner in a mountain restaurant.

the resort

eating out

If by now you're feeling that eating plays an as important role as skiing in Zermatt, you won't be too surprised that there are over 100 places to choose to dine in - not including the 40 or so mountain restaurants.

restaurants

Though it's difficult to get a cheap meal in Zermatt, it's not difficult to get a good one. A lot of the dishes on offer seem inspired by the chef's proximity to Italy - and hence to excellent Italian produce. There is some culinary loyalty - should your tastebuds be demanding rustic Swiss-French fare (fondues and raclettes) or Swiss-German sustenance (röstis and grilled meats) you can find both. In some places the food influences merge, such as Italian pasta and German sausage served with apple sauce... though it sounds strange it works. And if you're not convinced, you can also eat Japanese, Mexican, Thai, Chinese and even "Asian-fusion".

Being close to Italy also helps the wine list - choice is not restricted to the local Valais bouquets or over-priced imports, as decent Italian bottles are widely available and generally well priced.

Few of the restaurants in town open at **lunchtime** - probably realising that they'd lose the battle for clientele to their contemporaries on the mountain. The evening **service** can be short as well - some places close as early as 9:30pm, but you can start eating as early as 6pm. You will always need to **reserve** a table at the more popular restaurants at weekends and during peak weeks. If you are looking for a table on the off-chance, your best bet is later on in the evening when the bulk of the trade has eased. Many of the restaurants have a **terrace**, which is best enjoyed in the morning or early afternoon, before the sun slips behind the Matterhorn.

snapshot

best for...
something cheesy - ross-stall
flamboyance - le chalet dà giuseppe
entertainment - chez heini
lamb - le mazot
families - the pipe
romance - dorfbeizli
style - mood's
vegetarians - china garden
hot stuff - weisshorn

prices

The price per head for a main course (excluding drinks) is shown in each review:
£ below CHF10
££ CHF10-CHF20
£££ CHF20-CHF30
££££ CHF30-CHF40
£££££ above CHF40
Unless otherwise stated, all reviewed restaurants accept most credit cards.

eating out

restaurants
1. ross-stall
2. le mazot
3. chez heini
4. steak-house
5. la chalet dà giuseppe
6. china garden
7. weisshorn
8. mood's
9. pizzeria roma
10. the pipe
11. fuji's
12. dorfbeizli
13. casa portuguesa

cafés/take-away
14. café du pont
15. crêperie serac
16. mcdonald's
17. brown cow
18. party service
19. pizza flash
20. crêperie

food & drink

la chalet dà giuseppe

☎ 027 967 1380
🕐 6:30pm-11:30pm
✗ traditional italian

Situated in an unassuming looking building, away from the main drag, you could easily miss Giuseppe's if you don't know what you're looking for, which would be a shame as this is one of Zermatt's best. Though the sea-themed décor (of fishermen's nets and unlucky crustaceans) could do with an overhaul, it sets the scene for the menu - many of the dishes are fish based, such as the delicious garlic-enhanced gambas and perfectly cooked sea bass.

The Giuseppe of the restaurant's name is omnipresent - both in picture form on the menus and in the flesh. A consummate host he nearly always recognises those who have been before - and is rewarded for his hospitality by a loyal client base, who return year after year. Even if you're fit to bursting, the character and bonhomie of your host makes it difficult to say no to dessert (such as melt-in-the-mouth tiramisu and the lighter-than-air panacotta) and rude to say no to the bottle of firewater presented to each table. The restaurant's bar groans with dusty bottles of ominous looking digestifs (a description which probably understates their effect). It is best to book, possibly even before you arrive in resort. And one final warning, be careful of the dog that brings you your bill...

eating out

ross-stall £££

☎ 027 967 3040
⏲ 4pm-11pm
✕ fondue & raclette

p89 b1

The 'horse-place' or stable is the best place for a cheesy meal - at least in terms of the food available. The cheese fondues and raclette are the mainstays, though you can plump for the carnivore option. Service is very friendly and the staff are more than happy to explain the process, if you're a novice to this kind of DIY dining. On first sight it's a small venue, but there are also tables downstairs where larger parties can enjoy their own company without disturbing the guests upstairs.

the steak house £££

☎ 027 967 6700
⏲ 5pm-12am
✕ meat

p89 c1

The Steak-House or Zur Alten Mühle (the Old Mill) is one of the 4 restaurants run by the Walliserkanne hotel - the others being the China Garden, Il Ristorante and the hotel's own restaurant. The name is the main clue to the menu (not much originality there) as meat is the order of the day. You can choose from beef, venison, lamb or pork, served with french fries, baked potato, rice or corn on the cob - suitably filling fare after a day on the slopes. The restaurant can accommodate any lost non-meat eaters by getting vegetarian food from its Oriental cousin upstairs (the China Garden). Despite being underground, it is a well-lit venue and the wooden surrounds - kitschly decorated with ears of corn - add to the old farm feel.

china garden £££

☎ 027 967 5323
⏲ 12pm-2pm, 6pm-12am
✕ chinese

p89 c1

The only Chinese restaurant in Zermatt and not a bad attempt. While some of the combinations on the menu wouldn't immediately strike you as Chinese, there's enough to satisfy the urge for the Far East. Red lacquered furniture and black bamboo accessories complete the look of an emperor's temple. And though they have a slightly formulaic feel, the food and service are as well polished as the furniture.

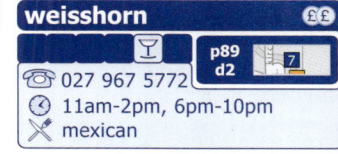

weisshorn ££

☎ 027 967 5772
⏲ 11am-2pm, 6pm-10pm
✕ mexican

p89 d2

Putting a spin on chilli in the alps, the Weisshorn is the place for something a little hotter. Suitably decorated in bold primary colours and Mexican sombreros, most of the menu is as you'd expect to find - tasty fajitas, enchiladas and tacos to eat and restorative margaritas, mojitos and pina coladas to drink. The

eating out

Weisshorn hedges its bets a little, serving rösti (one of the few in town places you can get it) and fondue, as well as afternoon tea (2pm-5pm).

mood's £££££
☎ 027 967 8484
🕓 6:30pm-11pm
✕ international
p89 d1 8

Argument rages as to whether you go to Mood's for the food or the style - and though Lynne Truss might put a question mark next to the apostrophe, some rate it as Zermatt's best for both. You can enjoy a pre (or post) dinner drink in the ground floor piano bar or upstairs in the nautically-themed Boathouse bar (➜ après-ski & nightlife). The restaurant is also upstairs, arranged in a series of stylishly furnished rooms with generously spaced tables. The food is European and contemporary - fish is a speciality - and the comprehensive wine list is as much of a feature, starting at a comfortably priced level and reaching as high as the surrounding peaks.

chez heini ££££
☎ 027 967 1630
🕓 6:30pm-10pm
✕ traditional swiss
p89 a3 3

Heini's is not a place you stumble across by chance as it is tucked away in Weisti. But its infamy (or at least that of the owner) means your taxi driver is likely to know where it is. Like many of the restaurants cooking local produce, Heini's prides itself on using lamb reared on the family farm - then cooked to perfection on an open fire. But what sets Heini's apart from the rest is the after dinner entertainment - from Dan Daniell, a local celeb and Heini's extrovert owner. With a CV listing a whole host of professions including singer, writer, cook, entertainer, philosopher, clothes designer and restaurateur, it is his skill as an entertainer you get to see - Daniell is fond of breaking into song after the dinner service (often in German with his own lyrics). The spontaneous karaoke makes up for the rather gloomy décor, which could do with updating - but despite this the formula seems to work, and bookings are essential.

pizzeria roma ££
☎ 027 967 3229
🕓 6:30pm-10:30pm
✕ wood fired pizza
p89 d4 9

One of the many Italian run restaurants in Zermatt, this one serves the dish that Italy is best known for - pizza. Cooked in a wood fired oven, you can be assured of a tasty result. And if you're happy to wait you can get a table without a reservation. The ambience is relaxed and friendly and a pleasant change from some of the more serious attitudes you might come across elsewhere in the resort's eateries.

eating out

the pipe ££

📞 079 758 5324
🕐 4pm-1am (2:30am on w/e)
🍴 fusion foods

p89 d2 — 10

Billed as a surfers cantina, the entrance to the Pipe is flanked by brightly coloured surf boards and the inside is populated by stereotypical seasonnaires. As surfers don't really have a cuisine type, the menu is an extensive range of "fusion foods" - anything from Sri-Lankan style curries to Caribbean Jambalayas (there are often theme nights to match the food). On Sundays, it opens at lunch-time and regularly serves a roast dinner for the home-sick English contingent - who will be made even happier by the 3 hour Sunday happy hour (5pm-8pm). There is a range of set menus for big groups - and with its reasonable prices it is a good option for your chalet boy's night off. However, once the à la carte service stops at 10:30pm, the Pipe crosses into altogether murkier and flavoured-vodka flavoured territory - though if you need something to counteract its effects a range of snacks is available until 1pm. Also home to the freeride film factory (t 079 213 3807) - you can be the star of your own skiing movie.

fuji's £££

📞 027 966 6171
🕐 11:30am-2pm, 6pm-12am
🍴 sushi, sashimi & teppanyaki

p89 e3 — 11

One of 2 restaurants in the resort serving Japanese food is found on the ground floor of the mock temple Albana Real hotel (the other is Myoko (t 027 966 8739) run by the Seiler family). If you are no longer charmed by the national obsession for cooking your own food, at Fuji's you can take pleasure in watching somebody cook it for you. Seating is arranged around two fiercely hot plates where you can watch the skilfully trained chefs prepare the teppanyaki à la carte menu. The fresh sushi and sashimi are also delicious and carefully prepared. It's best to book as there is only room for about 30 lucky diners, and this is also one of the few restaurants open for lunch.

dorfbeizli ££££

📞 027 968 1918
🕐 6:30pm-10:30pm
🍴 modern european

p89 e2 — 12

Though this cosy little restaurant is in the same building as the Matterhorn hostel (➥ hotels), that is the only similarity between the two. The menu includes a number of dishes incorporating horse, so if you think of equines more as friends than as fodder, choose carefully - the hostess is charming but speaks little English and the menu is not a work of perfect translation. Though the room is small, clever use of furniture and fittings and copious candles give it an intimate feeling perfect for swooning duos.

eating out

casa portuguesa ££

☎ 027 966 3030
🕐 11am-2pm, 6pm-10pm
✗ portugese

p89 a1

Somewhat out of the main action and something of a well kept secret, the aptly named Casa is home from home for many of the seasonal locals. Popular with the non-English resort staff, this is very much a gathering spot for the population of Macedonians, Croats and, of course, Portuguese. The menu includes delicacies such as salted cod, which you can wash down with either of Portugal's finest liquid exports - port or Super Bock beer while you soak up the down-to-earth atmosphere.

and the rest...

All of the hotels (but not the garnis) have a restaurant in which non-residents can also eat - the best is the **schäferstübli** (t 027 966 7605) in the hotel Julen and those in the Seiler-owned hotels have a generally good reputation. Those looking for a decent steak could try any one of the numerous grillrooms - 2 of the best are the **spycher** (t 027 967 7741/2041) on Steinmatte and the **stockhorn grillroom** (t 027 967 1747) in the Hotel Stockhorn. The Hotel Post on Bahnhofstrasse offers a variety of places to eat: at the **pizzeria broken** (6pm-1:30am) you can create your own pizza while the **old spaghetti factory** (6:30pm-11pm) serves the usual range of pasta-based dishes and the **restaurant portofino** (7pm-11pm) dishes up a good selection of Mediterranean and fish dishes. **grampi's** (t 027 967 7775), also on Bahnhofstrasse, is known for its chicken wings and ribs.

eating out

cafés

It's hard to move in Zermatt without tripping over a café. Cake is king. And a skiing holiday is the one time you don't feel guilty about letting it rule. While you won't get a tall skinny mochacino with soya milk to go, you will get a creamy hot chocolate or a super-sweet herbal tea. Most of the cafés are run by families and have been for a number of years - and one taste confirms the years of expertise. Café culture is very much established among the permanent residents and if you stay long enough you will notice the same people at the same table for the morning ritual of *"gipfel und kaffee"*. The cafés are also good places to seek refuge from the hectic après in the bars - or to recharge before you venture into the glühwein fuelled throng.

There isn't much difference between the leagues of cake-dispensing cafés. One of the best is the **tea-room darioli** (t 027 967 1895) - opposite the Bahnhof is often a hive of activity and a good place to people-watch excited arrivees and reluctant departees. The amusingly named **café fuchs** (t 027 967 2063) is a little off the beaten track, which makes it one of the few where you are guaranteed to get a seat, whatever the time of day. **tea-room biner** (t 027 967 6167) on the corner of Ufer Weg is a good place to shelter from the storm whilst waiting for the bus - alternatively, if the sun is shining, you can take your tissane on the terrace outside. There are 4 cafés on Bahnhofstrasse of which **café-conditorei zellner** (t 027 967 1855) is probably the best - with less spartan surroundings than some it is justifiably popular and the smiling waitresses deal slickly with the crowds. All of the cafés open in the early hours and stay open through the lunch-time siesta, so if you find your shopping trip abruptly cut short at midday when the shops close, they give you somewhere to while away the 2 hour break.

Of course if cake is not your thing, a few other places are café-like in atmosphere but savoury in flavour.

café du pont ££

☎ 027 967 4343
🕓 8am-10pm
✗ traditional snacks

p89 d2

Located on the south edge of the Kircheplatz, the Café du Pont is the oldest eatery in Zermatt - and both inside and out it looks like nothing much has been changed since it opened. Sitting somewhere between café and restaurant, the menu of omelettes, sandwiches and rösti covers both lunch and evening. It's an easy place to sit and watch the world go by and find out what the locals do with their day - most of them seem to spend it here.

eating out

crêperie serac £

☎ 027 967 1519
🕐 8am-10pm
🍴 crêpes

p89 c2

The only sit-down option for a crêpe. Optimistically billed as a bistro-café-bar, you are only likely to go for a pancake (savoury or sweet) - but that could be for breakfast, noon or afternoon tea, or any other time that seems appropriate. Situated on the same part of the strip as Stoked ski school and its hip streetwear shop, its décor is suitably modern. A big attraction is the street-side terrace - it is one of the few cafés to have one.

brown cow ££

☎ 027 967 1931
🕐 9am-2am
🍴 burgers & bar snacks

p89 d2

For more substantial fare than a pancake and less Swiss fare than a fondue, the Brown Cow serves a decent range of bar snacks, including burgers and salads. And despite its position as the ringleader of Zermatt's après scene, the vibe during the day is more chilled out and relaxing - in fact if you haven't seen it it's hard to imagine that the bar is transformed into a mass of beer-downing crowds when the clock strikes après o'clock. Before then you can enjoy your food in relative peace while watching music videos on the various TVs dotted around.

mcdonald's £

☎ 027 967 6465
🕐 9am-11pm
🍴 mcdonald's

p89 c1

Hard to call it a restaurant and hard to call it a café, this place may have a feel and a look that you recognise. Its range of burgers (and even salads) doesn't attract the health conscious and the décor won't please the traditionlists, but the service is the quickest in town and your bill will be one of the smallest you get.

eating out

late night & take-away

The only type of food available late at night is pizza - either from the Hotel Post or from GramPi's until 1:30am, so you need to make sure your hunger pangs coincide with being close to one of them. If you are staying in and can't be bothered to cook, a few places will let you take-away and a couple will accommodate any real sloth by bringing it to you.

For a resort that prides itself on the quality and quantity of its mountain restaurants the idea of lunch on the run is almost an insult. This probably explains the scarcity of places where you can take-away food between 12pm-2am - not all of the bakeries or supermarkets stay open over lunch-time, forcing you to plan ahead or to sit down somewhere.

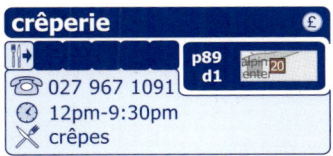

crêperie £

☎ 027 967 1091
🕓 12pm-9:30pm
🍴 crêpes

p89 d1

Operating from a small window next door to the Little Bar, the Crêperie is good for those looking for a late lunch on the move. A range of delicious crêpes are available - for something savoury try the cheese and spinach and for a sweet tooth the banana and chocolate combo is heavenly. You can eat them at the small counter - useful if you're not sure if one is going to be enough.

party service ££

☎ 027 967 1938
🕓 9am-1pm, 5pm-9pm
🍴 pizza & deli

p89 a3

Party Service's location on the south edge of Wiesti means you are unlikely to pass by on the way home. Fortunately they will deliver their take-away pizza (available with a variety of toppings) and deli platters - the choice ranges from the Norwegan option (smoked salmon and trout) to something more local, the Valaisanne (a hearty selection of meats and cheese). Handy if you miss the supermarket or for an impromptu party.

pizza flash ££

☎ 027 967 2121
🕓 6pm-11pm
🍴 pizza

p89 c2

Another take-away pizza option is the Vieux-valais Pizzeria or "Pizza Flash" on Hofmattstrasse. You can also take-away pasta and a range of drinks (including wine and beer) and they also deliver.

après-ski & nightlife

Zermatt's après-ski will soon help you get rid of any excess energy. The focus is on having a good time, whatever your poison. That's not to say you can't find somewhere quiet for a drink to ease you into the evening, but if that's what you're looking for you're probably missing the point. The après scene starts as soon after lunch as is socially acceptable, both in town and on the mountain. Indeed après is such a big part of the Zermatt experience that many skiers forgo the shower and snooze option after skiing and go from bar to bar to restaurant to bar to bar to club to bed in their skiing best.

In town the popular venues are concentrated along Bahnhofstrasse and Steinmattstrasse and by late afternoon the bars and pubs are full of red-faced skiers seeking to recount the tales of the day over a few beers. Tales (and beer-drinking) continue without respite until 3:30am.

bars & pubs

In a pleasant change from some other resorts, both are run and staffed by locals as well as season workers - though the language of beer is universally recognised so you don't need to worry that you won't get what you order. Many of the **hotels** have bars, which welcome non-residents as well as guests - opening times fluctuate, the bars generally staying open until the last drinker leaves.

snapshot

après...
classic après - brown cow
ski boots de rigeur - papperla
sing-along - hennustall

après après...
cocktail hour - papa caesar's
aphrodisiacs - elsie's bar
swiss chic - mood's

& dawn-breakers
party people - the barrel
chilled cool - vernissage

There isn't really a **timetable** to the week. If you're looking for loud and lively you can find it most nights, and most afternoons on the slopes - a testament to the stamina of the resort's visitors.

prices

Liquid refreshment doesn't come cheap no matter where you go - a spirit and mixer costs around CHF10 and a cocktail CHF15. Beer is the cheapest at about CHF5 for a half litre. And as with anywhere else, buying wine by the bottle is more cost effective - as long as you can drink it all.

après-ski & nightlife

bars & pubs
1. hotel post the village the broken
2. papperla
3. mood's
4. the north wall
5. montrose bar
6. vernissage
7. z'alt hischi
8. the country bar
9. the little bar
10. elsie's bar
11. grampi's
12. hotel alex

nightclubs
13. schneewittchen

99

copyright qanuk 2004

après-ski & nightlife

hotel post

☎ 027 967 1931
🕒 opening hours vary

The Post is a difficult place to pigeonhole. Zermatt's best known and most well-established entertainment venue, most people go there to drink - and the choice of where is extensive. For somewhere noisy and steamy try the **brown cow** (9am-2pm) on the ground floor - you can watch live sports and music videos whilst downing a large draught beer. For the more sophisticated, **papa caesar's** cocktail lounge (the first name of a former owner rather than a nod to the Roman Empire) on the first floor serves decent cocktails in a ambient and laid-back setting (6pm-2am, happy hour 7pm-8pm). **the pink** (9pm-2am) is home to a piano of the same colour and is for aficionados of live music, from jazz to rock (played by bands from as far afield as the USA and Jamaica).

For those with more interest in sustenance than schnapps, the choice is as broad - and if a heady mix of food and drink is not enough, you can shake it up some more in one of the Post's danceries - the **broken bar-disco** or the **village dance club** (➙ nightclubs).

The hardest thing to do in the Post is leave... literally. With so many venues, there are a lot of doors, which may double after some après - a carafe of wine at dinner, a few digestifs and a few shots can make it hard to figure out which exit is the exit.

après-ski & nightlife

papperla

☎ 027 967 4040
⏰ 12pm-12am

p99 d3 [2]

Although the Papperla is open until late, it comes into its own as the ski lifts close. Ski suited and booted holiday makers descend on the street-side terrace, which with its reverberating pop music and patio heaters is a lively and warm place to re-hydrate without too much effort at the end of the skiing day. A great place to people-watch and to work out whether all-in-ones are making a comeback.

mood's

☎ 027 967 8484
⏰ 5pm-2am

p99 d1 [3]

Known as Mood's and as the Pink Elephant, the latter is a more obvious name. But don't be put off by the monstrously florid beast by the entrance (a theme continued less obtrusively inside) as it belies the chic interior. The mood-themed menu - such as champagne cocktails if you're feeling flamboyant or tequila shooters if you're feeling furious - should get you in the, err, mood. The surprisingly good pianist should help enhance it further, and once you've sunk into the comfy leather couches and warmed yourself in front of the glass-walled fire, you can only be in a good one. From the lounge area you can glimpse the restaurant's kitchen at work, which may leave you hungrier for more than just nibbles. Sailors can also take their tipple in the Boathouse Bar upstairs (home to the Zermatt Yacht, Golf and Country Club) and wonder how often the Zamoura of Zermatt (the yacht outside) gets to see the sea.

north wall

☎ 027 966 3412
⏰ 6:30pm-12am

p99 e3 [4]

Something of a seasonnaires' hang out, the North Wall caters for its clientele accordingly - with daily drinks promotions and pizza and nachos to fill a hole. Add to this the large screen showing extreme videos and it ticks all the boxes. As Zermatt has a small community of seasonnaires, they will know if you're not one.

montrose bar

☎ 027 966 0333
⏰ all day

p99 d1/2 [5]

A tiny bar on the ground floor on the hotel Monte Rosa and in the same cosy vein. Traditional and unpretentious, the bar takes more than just its name from Scotland - the room itself is an explosion of tartan and provides a great escape from the winter chill. And a wee dram from the obligatory line-up of single malts will soon warm you up. A visit also gives you the perfect excuse to have a look around Zermatt's oldest hotel and soak up the nostalgic atmosphere.

après-ski & nightlife

vernissage

☎ 027 967 6636
⏲ 11am-2am

p99 c2

Another one-stop shop but in an entirely different style to the in-yer-face Post. The interior is modern, unfailingly contemporary and inspired by the world of film - such as the chandeliers in the bar. The bar and lounge area are on the first (lower) level, reached by a curved staircase that you half expect a movie star to shimmy down. Filled with comfy leather sofas, the mood lighting helps everybody look beautiful - as do the well-mixed cocktails. The floor beneath the bar is home to the gallery - the closest you'll come to cultural hob-nobbing - as well as the cinema auditorium. Despite its arthouse looks, the films are definitely mainstream - a mix of recent and older releases. And Vernissage's movie and dinner option lets you catch a flick, feed your hunger and quench your thirst all at the same time. From 10pm every night, cinema becomes club - and one with a chilled out vibe where the young and hip shake their collective thang.

z'alt hischi

☎ 027 967 4262
⏲ 5pm-2am

p99 c2

If you're looking for something a little stronger, Z'alt Hischi is the place to head to. A favourite with the locals, it doesn't need a happy hour, because the measures of spirits served are huge. Little attention is paid to the décor - less here is most definitely more, the more being in your glass. Hidden down the narrow Hinterdorfstrasse (a fragrant street that is also affectionately known as cat-piss alley) the brave can try the home-made egg liqueur and start the descent on a different slippery slope... into oblivion.

country bar

☎ 027 967 1596
⏲ 10am-12am

p99 c2

The kind of place where doors creak, heads turn and the dust slowly settles when you walk in. The Country Bar almost seems surprised to get clientele - but once they've got over the shock, the nearest you'll get to a cowboy is a hustler at one of its pool tables. Otherwise you can keep yourself entertained with the table football or one of the 21 internet terminals.

little bar

☎
⏲ 5pm-2am

p99 d1

The clue is in the name - this sub-terranean drinking den reaches capacity with about 20 people, so it's not somewhere for the claustrophobic. But it only takes a handful of drinkers to make it a party - if you're in a big group you

après-ski & nightlife

can make it your own. The "little" could also apply to the seeming lack of care and attention given to the décor - there is little more to it than the unadorned cellar walls and flagstone floors. But despite the rather gloomy inside, the cosiness of the space once filled transforms it into quite a cheery place.

elsie's bar

☎ 027 967 2431
🕓 11am-2am
p99 d2

Elsie's is the epicure's choice - a bottle of champagne and a dozen oysters (French or Irish) is a commonly heard order, though for the less extravagant the hot chocolate (a house speciality) is a good option. Zermatt must attract lovers of aphrodisiacs as Elsie's 3 floors are rarely quiet - tables are rather snug, so you need to be feeling convivial and it's not somewhere to go for a private conversation or a guaranteed seat. And though the cosily cramped interior may look like somewhere Shakespeare would have chosen to pen his latest blockbuster, the atmosphere is pure ski resort - albeit at the pricer end of the scale.

grampi's

☎ 027 967 7775
🕓 5pm-2am
p99 d1

GramPi's is the Post's main competitor - at least in terms of location as it is situated directly opposite on Bahnhofstrasse. Like the Post, GramPi's goes for the all-things-for-all-people approach, but unlike the Post it only offers one of each - 1 bar, 1 restaurant and 1 dancefloor. The bar on the ground floor is unpretentious and the nearest you'll get to an Irish pub. The restaurant on the first floor is low-key and perfect for easy dining on pizza and pasta. And the dance floor in the basement should be able to accommodate your toes should they start tapping. And if you want some post-dancing nosh, you can take away a pizza until late. GramPi's has the same owner as the witch-festooned Hexenbar (decorations rather than clientele), just across the street.

hotel alex

☎ 027 966 7090
🕓 all day
p99 c1

The lobby in the hotel Alex is a theme bar with a difference. The central hub of bar is surrounded by several individually decorated crannies from the Scottish-inspired "Highlander" nook to the holier-than-thou and sugary sweet "Angel's Corner". For sunnier days, you can escape from the eclectic mix of décor to the winter garden at the front of the hotel - a large terrace enclosed by stained glass surrounds (a material used extensively throughout the hotel), which being away from Bahnhofstrasse is a relaxed oasis of calm.

103

après-ski & nightlife

and the rest
The **kegelbahn** (t 027 663 366) in the basement of the hotel Bristol has the atmosphere of a working men's club and offers bowling, table football and alcohol to keep you amused. Upstairs the hotel has a slightly more formal bar. Options on the hill include the **hennustall** (t 079 213 3669) in the early evening or **olympia** (t 027 967 2407) for both early and late. For music aficionados, many of the hotels have piano bars - try the **butterfly** (t 027 966 4166) or the **beau-site** (t 027 966 6868) - or live music at the **schwyzer stübli** in the hotel Schweizerhof (t 027 966 0000).

nightclubs
While the distinction between bar and disco tends to blur in most of the night-time venues, the bars proper are closed by 2am. The nightclubs true are open to 4am to entertain those not so keen to catch the first lift. Clubbing in Zermatt is much like in any other ski resort and the DJs see no shame in playing a mix of cheesy music, with the odd top 40 hit thrown in for good measure - or by sheer luck. The outside temperature is cooler than the late night scene - you will see many 'moves' your dad would be proud of. Some of the hotels have their own discos (such as the hotel Alex) for those who like their bed to be within stumbling distance. None of the clubs have a dress policy so there's no need to dig out the glad rags - you're as well as off in your ski gear as your party frock, though ski boots might get in the way of some fancy footwork.

prices
No surprises - drinks are expensive. the pay-off for being able to drink yourself silly into the small hours is that your tipple has an inflated price. Spirits can be bought by the bottle and mixers are then provided free - if you are part of a group (or will go back most nights) this works out fairly good value.

après-ski & nightlife

village dance club

☎ 027 967 1931
🕘 9pm-4am
p99 d2

The name is about the only similarity to a local dance-hall. This is Zermatt's most 'trendy' club and those in the know congregate to shake their booty in the old alpine barn that is known as the Village. DJs are touted as "international", and overall the music is a thankful departure from the eurotrash often played elsewhere - house and R&B tend to get the most airplay here. Though the darkened gloom can make it hard to tell which of the Post's nightclubs you are in, the Village has a less claustrophobic feel than the Broken - and employs leather sofas, farming relics and a few potted plants as decoration. Those concerned with keeping up appearances can be assured they have made the choice of the 'in-crowd' - though at this end of the day will you really care?

broken bar-disco

☎ 027 967 1931
🕘 9pm-4am
p99 d2

In the basement of the Post is the Broken bar-disco. Probably the only club in the world that has a world-famous barrel - not for storing the beer but for dancing on, an activity which is strangely compelling after a few schnapps. The Broken is somewhere even the tone deaf can unashamedly air their vocal chords - as any mis-hit notes will be drowned out by the collective chorus singing along to classic hit after classic hit.

schneewittchen

☎ -
🕘 9pm-3am
p99 d3

Below the Papperla Pub the Schneewittchen is the embodiment of a ski resort nightclub. Very much a 'disco' the music is universally europop, age is not a bar to participation on the dancefloor and it's not unusual to see the re-enactment of Whigfield-type dance routines. And the Schneewittchen wins the prize for most entertaining use of the Matterhorn - a large image of the pristine peak is used as the backdrop to the scantily clad dancers that grace the stage from time-to-time. Not so snow white.

and the rest

If you're looking for something a bit more regional **dancing simi** at the hotel Simi (t 027 966 4600) offers a blend of Swiss folk and oompah music (and some pop) Tuesdays-Saturdays (9pm-3am).

activities

When the lifts are closed because of too little or - more frustratingly - too much snow, there a few things to keep you occupied.

more exercise?
While there is no municipal, a number of Zermatt's hotels have **swimming pools** (at the Biner, the Christiania, the Eden and the Schweizerhof), open to non-residents for a small charge. Of these, the biggest pool is at the Hotel Christiania open 8am-10.30am and 2pm-8pm, CHF10 for adult and CHF for children. For a different kind of workout, regular aerobics classes are held in the **sports hall** (triftbachhalle) behind the Zermatterhof hotel. For a gentle stretch rather than an energetic workout, you can always seeks out the resort's only **bowling alley** (kegelbahn) (t 027 966 3380, closed Sundays). In the basement of the Hotel Bristol this is almost a relic compared to the more modern bowling complexes you may be used to at home. There are only 2 lanes, but despite this you can normally get one (or both). If you have to wait you can amuse yourself with a drink at the bar or at the darts board or table football.

Zermatt has a huge **ice-skating** rink, well situated in the middle of the village, just behind Bahnhofstrasse. Though don't leave it to March or April to don steel-bladed shoes, as the rink is likely to have melted away to become several football pitches. You can also have a go at **curling** (t 027 967 3673, daily in December and January 10am-4pm) on the rink - or watch the experts.

For those fearing they will slip down the ladder at home the hotel Alex (t 027 966 7070) has **squash** courts, which are open to non-residents as well as residents. For those with Wimbledon aspirations, the hotel also has indoor **tennis** courts, as does the Alpenresort hotel (t 027 966 3000). Make sure you reserve, as you are unlikely to be able to simply turn up and play.

the sky's the limit
If you want to see the snow-capped peaks and glaciers from a different perspective, you can strap on some wings and take to the skies, by **parapenting** with the Air-Born Flight School (t 027 967 6744). If you want to be high but warm, Air Zermatt (t 027 966 8686, i air-zermatt.ch) runs **sightseeing flights** by helicopter or plane (for a minimum of 4 people) around the Matterhorn. If you want to be high but on terra firma, try the **panorama platform** at the top of the Klein Matterhorn. It's an altogether cheaper alternative to the airborne options, and you don't have to worry about not being able to take off.

The sky is also the limit for **shopaholics** - who can content themselves with watches, clothes (for skiing and for less practical purposes) as well as art and jewellery, including the

activities

blue lapis lazuli a semi-precious stone found around the area, and more unusual products such as marmot grease - supposedly good for a number of ailments! The **casino** (t 027 966 8181, i casino.zermatt.ch) in the hotel Zermatterhof will relieve any heavy wallets by means of American roulette, blackjack and the more instantly gratifying slot machines. Open 6pm-3am, dress like you can afford to be there.

take a geography lesson
The **peak collection** at the top of the Rothorn is, as the name suggests, a collection of rocks taken from around the region and displayed with explanations about the geography. The **glacier palace** at the Klein Matterhorn is the highest in the world (3820m). 15m below the surface is a world (or underworld) of a glacier, complete with crevasses, sculptures, information on their about geology. Open 9am-3pm entrance is free.

culture vulture
The hotel Mont Cervin has a programme of **classical music concerts** from Mozart to Chopin, Beethoven to Bach every so often in the evening (CHF 45), as does the main church on Kircheplatz - look for the flyers around the town.

The **alpine museum** pays homage to the history of climbing and tourism in Zermatt, including Edward Whymper's ascent of the Matterhorn and the geology and natural history of the alpine area. Ooen 4:30pm-6:30pm Mondays to Fridays children under 16 are free. Vernissages's **cinema** (t 027 967 6636, i vernissage-zermatt.ch) has 2 showings a day - either international movies or films about the mountains.

body beautiful
After a few days of brutal bruising courtesy of the slopes, your body may be in need of some tlc. For **massages** try the Saxifraga sauna and massage centre (t 079 607 6961/027 967 2792), open 4pm-10pm during the week or the Top-Fit health center (t 027 967 6120) in the Viktoria Center. A number of hotels have in-house masseurs - the most luxurious of which is the Clarins Spa (t 027 966 8888) in the hotel Mont Cervin which offers a range of health treatments. A number of hotels have **saunas** and **steam baths** (including the Christania, the Eden and the Biner) which are open to non-residents for a small charge. The Arca Solebad Aparthotel has a salt water pool at a particularly soothing 33°C.

further afield
The Zermatt to Davos **glacier express** (i glacierexpress.ch) is a scenic journey by train on a narrow-gauge railway. Passing from one to the other over the Oberalp Pass and the glitz of St. Moritz, it takes 8½ hours. Just don't think of Agatha Christie as the almost toy train disappears into the dark tunnels.

children

Given the limitations of the ski area for children, Zermatt has a surprisingly good range of facilities. With all you need to book well ahead as spaces are limited - particularly for the ski schools during the school holidays.

a word of caution

Children can find it difficult to adapt to the thinner air at high altitude, particularly when coupled with the excitement of all that cold white stuff. The ever-sensible Swiss are well aware of this and will not allow children aged 3 and under to go to the top of the Klein Matterhorn - so don't make that part of your itinerary.

tour operators

Most of the tour opeators offer discounted or free child places in their chalets and will provide a special children's meal. **simply ski** run a private nanny service during the day in your chalet (if you reserve the whole chalet). The nanny can look after up to 3 children (aged 6 months-8 years) at any one time. **ski scott dunn** also have private nannies to look after the children in their chalet (from 6 months upwards) - though you must book this service before departure. **powder byrne** offers a crèche all season for children aged 6 months-3 years and a variety of ski clubs (from mid- February until the end of the season) for children aged 4-14 years. They also run an Easter ski camp with ex-British skier Martin Bell for 11-15 year olds. A babysitting services (at extra cost) is also available.

in-resort

Most hotels in resort do not charge for children aged under 5. Children aged between 6-12 years normally only pay 50% if they stay in the same room as their parents and 2 of them have **kindergartens**. The 4* Nicoletta (t 027 966 0777, i zermatt.ch/nicoletta) on Hofmattstrasse is one of the best equipped for children. Its kindergarten - the Nico Kids Club - is open Mondays-Fridays. Children aged 2-8 years can be left for a full day (9am-5pm) or half day (9am-1pm or 1pm-5pm). Priority is given to hotel guests and guests staying in any of the other Seiler owned hotels (at no charge). If there's space, the club is available to non-residents. Activities throughout the day range from painting, sledding, baking to a ride in horse-drawn carriage. The 4* La Ginabelle hotel (t 027 966 5000, i la.ginabelle.ch) has the Kinderclub Pumuckel which takes children from 2½ years of age. The tourist office keeps a list of independent **babysitters** - the average hourly rate is CHF 20.

Elsewhere in the resort the Kinderparadies (t 027 967 7252/079 679 5907, i kinderparadies-zermatt.ch) on the road from the Bahnhof to Spiss is a large, well-designed kindergarten with its own garden. Care is available for a full day or a half day (including or excluding lunch) and they will take

children

children 3 months-6 years. Open 7 days a week from 9am-5pm all the carers are qualified and speak good English. Entertainment in the afternoon includes sledding and walks. The kindergarten is popular so book well ahead - though if there is space, you can make a reservation up to the evening of the day before you want to leave your kids.

Zermatt has one of the most children-favourable **lift passes** - being free to children aged 9 and under. And there are a couple of childrens' ski areas with special slopes and lifts for smaller skiers - the best is at at Riffelberg on the Gornergrat. For **ski school** lessons, Stoked runs the Snowflakes Club - group lessons for children aged 4-12 years Mondays-Fridays for a half (2 hours) or a full day (4 hours, plus an hour for lunch). Stoked also has a kindergarten (for newcomers to skiing aged 3-12) called the Snowflakes Kids club. The nursery is at Schwarzsee at the top of the Matterhorn-Express gondola and children can be left for a full day (9:30-3:30pm with lunch) or a half day (9:30am-12pm). Learning to ski, in a safe and protected area, is the main activity. For children aged under 13, the SSS has the Snowli kindergarten open to 4-6 year olds Mondays-Fridays and Snowboard Kids. They also run full day ski lessons for children aged 6-12 years old Mondays-Fridays. The cost of lessons does not include a lift pass. As the majority of them place on the main pistes, all children must have a pass (even if this is just to show they can use the lifts for free).

Children must wear a helmet to join a group lesson. Make sure it fits well - children's heads don't grow as quickly as their body, so they should be able to use it for a couple of years (as long as it doesn't sustain any damage). You can buy an animal cover to make it more appealing.

Children can participate in the snow-based **activities** such as torchlit skiing. Off the snow one of the best is the Zermatt trampoline (t 079 214 3270) based at the sports arena behind Bahnhofstrasse. Open every afternoon 1:30pm-7pm the trampoline can bounce children aged 2 years and bigger 'kids' weighing in at no more than 90kg. The Vernissage **cinema** shows a childrens' film when the weather is bad enough to close most of the lifts.

seasonnaires

before you go

Before you decide what kind of job you want you need to decide what kind of season you want - a job as a rep will be better paid but you have more responsibility, while a job as a chalet host means fixed hours, but once you know the routine, more time to make the most of resort life. Most of the UK ski companies recruit seasonal workers - interviewing normally starts in May, though there may still be vacancies as late as December. Either contact the companies directly (not forgetting smaller or overseas based ones) or go through a recruitment website such as **natives.co.uk** - who have a comprehensive database of available jobs as well as a lot of information on everything about "doing a season" - **findaskijob.com** or **snowsportrecruitment.com**. It's a competitive market for jobs and while it is not essential, speaking reasonable German will help.

If you haven't got a job by October, it's worth going to the Ski Show at Olympia - some tour operators have a stall there as do Natives. If you haven't got a job by the start of the season, it can be worth heading out to the resort (if you can support yourself for a bit). Some of the less glamourous jobs may still be available and you will also get known - so when there is the inevitable fall-out of recruits due to unsuitability, New Year flu and mid-season blues, you can step into the role. Jobs constantly become available throughout the season - the ski market is very transient. Once employed most companies organise your **work permit**, **travel** to and from the resort, **accommodation**, **lift pass** and **equipment rental**. Most seasonnaire jobs come with a shared room as part of the package. If accommodation doesn't come with your job - or if you aren't planning on having a job - you would be well advised to find some digs before you head out. Accommodation is hard to find and you need to start looking as early as the summer. To work legally in Switzerland, you must have a work permit. The rules change on a regular basis - presently the permit is applied for by the employer but belongs to the employee, valid for employment anywhere in Switzerland, for any company for the length of its validity. If you are planning to DIY you should be aware that Zermatt has the most expensive lift pass in Europe.

once you're there

Zermatt's English or English-speaking seasonnaire population is small compared to resorts such as Chamonix or Verbier, mainly due to the small number of UK tour companies operating in the resort. This can give the community more of a family atmosphere - with only 120 people to get to know in a fairly small space - and many seasonnaires return year after year after decade. Conversely, it is not the resort for those who don't like living in a very

seasonnaires

small pond. The resort has enough **happy hours** that you can survive without getting special seasonnaire prices. There is a bit of covert discounting, depending upon how well you get to know the staff. With such a small community there aren't many officially organised evenings for seasonnaires, but there are plenty of ad hoc parties. Popular bars among the seasonnaire population include the North Wall, Vernissage and the Pipe. Trips to Olympia are also a feature (though you might bump into some of your clients). Club nights at the Post (such as the Ibiza winter season) and the Stoked ski school party are also highlights of the social calendar.

As Zermatt is a year-round place and so much more than just a ski resort, you should find everything you need - laundries, supermarkets and even a library should you be taking the winter off to catch up on your reading. If you have good intentions to learn something while you're there - and capitalise on it early on before they disappear in a haze of schnapps - the language school Julen (t 027 967 7222, i sprachschulejulen.com) runs courses for all levels in German, French, Italian and Spanish.

Calls home are expensive from an English **mobile**, so it could be worth investing in a Swiss SIM card and calls made within and out of Switzerland will be cheaper and you won't pay to receive calls from the UK. Check that your phone is 'unlocked' (so you can insert a foreign SIM card into it) before you leave the UK. You then pay as you go as you would in the UK. Top up cards are available from most of the newsagents in the resort. Orange is the best network for international calls, as it charges by the second rather than the minute. There are numerous **internet** points as well - the Country Club has 21 terminals so you rarely have to wait. The Stoked internet corner will let you plug in your own laptop for a small fee.

For full details of what's going on in and around the resort, you can rely on the official channels such as the Zermatt TV or radio Info Mattertal (97.8FM) both of which broadcast information on the ski area (lifts, pistes and weather reports) and events in and around the town. For less official news there's always the seasonnaire grapevine.

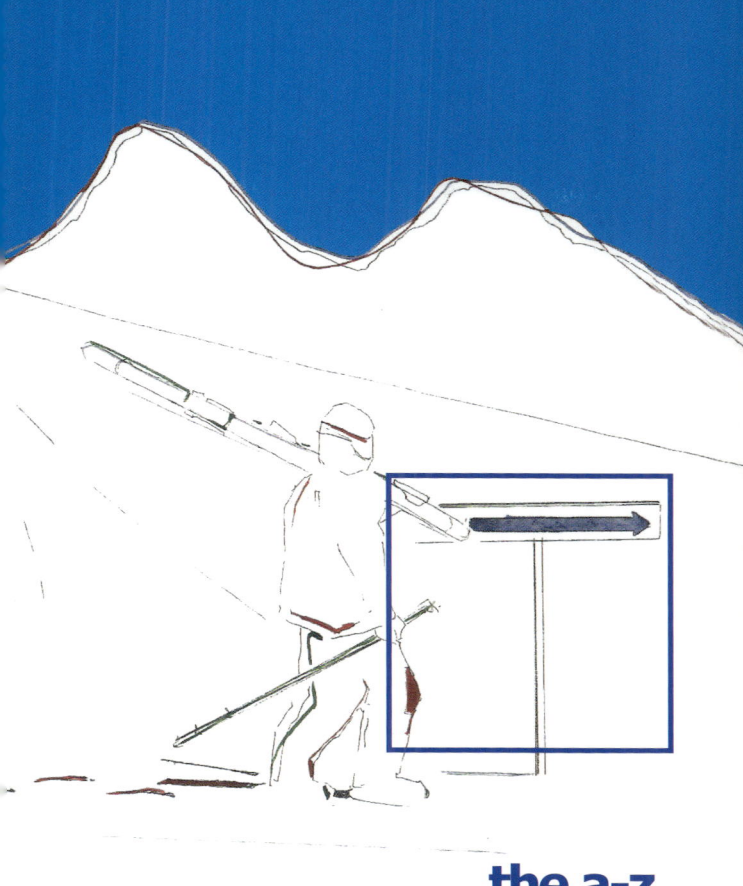

the a-z

tour operators

A list of the English based tour operators offering a range of accommodation in Zermatt. Though many of them offer a variety of different ways to take a skiing holiday they have been categorised according to their main strength.

highstreet
crystal t 0870 160 6040, i crystalski.co.uk
first choice t 0870 754 3477, i fcski.co.uk
inghams t 020 8780 4433, i inghams.co.uk
thomson t 0870 606 1470, i thomson-ski.co.uk

ski-specific
lotus supertravel t 027 204 4699, i supertravel.co.uk
simply ski t 0208 541 2209, i simplytravel.co.uk
ski club of great britain t 020 8410 2022, i skiclub.co.uk
ski independence t 0870 600 1462, i ski-independence.co.uk
ski with julia t 01386 584478, i skiwithjulia.co.uk

chalets only
total ski t 08701 633 633, i skitotal.com

children
powder byrne t 020 8246 5300, i powderbyrne.co.uk

luxury
elegant resorts t 01244 897 333, i elegantresorts.co.uk
ski scott dunn t 020 8682 5050, i scottdunn.com

self-catering & budget
interhome t 020 8891 1294, i interhome.co.uk
into mountains i intomountains.com

self-drive
drive alive t 0114 292 2971, i drive-alive.co.uk
erna low t 0207 584 2841, i ernalow.co.uk

tailor-made & weekends
made to measure holidays t 0124 353 3333, i madetomeasureholidays.com
momentum ski t 0207 371 9111, i momentum.uk.com
mountain exposure t 020 8692 7185, i mountainexposure.com
ski weekend t 0870 060 0615, i skiweekend.com
white roc ski weekends t 0207 792 1188, i whiteroc.co.uk

If you run a ski company that offers holidays to Zermatt but are not listed here, let us know by email to comments@snowmole.com and we will include you in the next edition of this guide.

directory

listings

All 027, 024, 022, 031 and 061 numbers need the Swiss international prefix (0041) if dialled from the UK.

transport

air
bmibaby t 0870 264 2229,
i bmibaby.com
british airways t 0870 850 9850,
i ba.com
easyjet t 0870 600 0000, i easyjet.co.uk
swiss t 0845 601 0956 i swiss.com
basel t 061 325 3111,
i euroairport.com
bern t 031 964 0919,
i flughafenbern.ch
sion t 027 329 0600, i sionairport.ch
geneva t 022 717 7111, i gva.ch
milan (linate & malpensa) t 0039 274 852 200, i sea-aeroportimilano.it
zurich t 043 816 2211. i zurich-airport.com

car hire
alamo i alamo.com
avis i avis.com
easycar t 0906 333 3333, i easycar.com
europcar i europcar.com
hertz t 0870 844 8844 i hertz.co.uk

driving
general - carry a valid driver's licence, proof of ownership, your insurance certificate and an emergency triangle.
road information - i viamichelin.com, t 163, 24/7 road assistance t 140
speed limits - in villages and suburbs the speed limit is 50km/h (unless indicated). The limit is 80km/h on all other roads and 120km/h on motorways.
signs & rules - motorway signs are

directory

green and you need a vignette (a windscreen sticker) to travel on them - buy one at the border. They last for the year in which bought and cost CHF40. You must wear a seatbelt in the front and back of a car. Children under 12 must sit in the back and babies and young children must be placed in special baby/young child seats. Important rules for driving in the mountains are that ascending vehicles have priority and postal buses and pedestrians always have right of way. A handbook on road signs and regulations is available in English from the cantonale police.

helicopter
air zermatt t 027 966 8686 i air-zermatt.ch

horse-drawn carriage/sleigh
t 079 436 7612

international train
raileurope t 0870 584 8848
i raileurope.co.uk
eurostar t 0870 518 6186
i eurostar.com
TGV i tgv.com

local train
rail service t 0900 300 300,
i railway.ch, cff.ch, rail.ch
täsch station - t 027 967 1214
täsch-zermatt train t 027 927 7777,
i mgbahn.ch, bvz.ch
bergbahnen t 027 966 0101, i zermatt-bergbahnen.ch

luggage service t 027 921 4560 (Täsch) or t 027 921 4611 (Zermatt)
gornergrat train t 027 921 4711,
i ggb.ch

maps
The tourist office has A4-sized maps of the village. Maps (1:50000 or 1:25000) of the surrounding area are available from Wega on Bahnhofstrasse.

parking
There are numerous garages in Täsch such as welcome parking (t 027 967 0170, i welcomeparking.ch) which cost approx. CHF15 per day. Some also offer a taxi service to Zermatt (see below). There is also (slightly cheaper) uncovered parking at Täsch station.

private minibus
alp line t 0033 677 865282, i alp-line.com
alpine cab i alpinecab.com.
ats t 0709 209 7392, i a-t-s.net

taxis
to/from täsch
alphubel t 027 967 1550, i alphubel.ch
christophe (24 hour) t 027 967 3535,
i st-christophe.com
eden t 027 967 6444
fredy t 027 967 3366
around zermatt
bolero t 027 967 6060
imboden t 027 967 7777
schaller t 027 967 1212

directory

health & safety

accidents
If you have an accident on the slopes, you will be taken to the nearest doctor unless you specify a particular one. To confirm you can pay for treatment carry a credit card and your insurance details. At some point, contact your insurance company to check whether they want to arrange your transport home. And ask your doctor for a medical certificate confirming you are fit to travel. If you see an accident on the slopes, tell the nearest rescue centre, normally at the top or bottom of lifts.

doctors
There are 5 surgeries - Bannwart, t 027 967 1188, Bieler, Brönnimann and Imoberdorf, t 027 967 4477, Julen t 027 967 6717, Lutz t 027 967 1916 and Stoessel, t 027 967 7979. They operate an emergency rota - available from the tourist office. The nearest hospitals are in Visp and Brig.

emergency numbers
air zermatt/ambulance t 027 966 8686, 144
fire brigade t 118
pistes SOS t 027 966 0100
police (distress call) t 117
cantonale police t 027 966 6920 (Bahnhofplatz, Mondays-Fridays 10am-12pm, 4pm-5:45pm)
municipal police (lost property) t 027 966 2222 (Haus Trifthorn, Mondays-Fridays 8am-10am, 5pm-6pm).

euro emergency t 112
Emergency calls are not always free from a phone box so you may need some change to make the call.

health
UK visitors don't need any vaccinations to enter Switzerland. There isn't a national health service, so you pay for treatment when you receive it.

insurance
Personal insurance covering wintersports and the cost of ambulances, helicopter rescue and emergency repatriation is essential as all these services are expensive. Policies differ greatly - some exclude off-piste skiing or cover it only if you go with a guide, so check the terms and conditions carefully. Also ensure that après-ski activities, such as sledging are covered. If you haven't arranged cover before you get to Zermatt you can buy an Air Zermatt card (t 027 966 8686, i airzermatt.ch) for CHF30 (or CHF 70 for a family package) from the Alpin Center or any of the lift pass offices. This is valid throughout Switzerland for a year and insures you against all rescue costs, helicopter transfer or transport deemed necessary.

pharmacies
3 in total - Internationale t 027 966 2727, Testa Grigia t 027 966 4949, Vital t 027 967 6677 - Mondays-Saturdays 8am-12pm, 2pm-7pm, Sundays and public holidays 10am-12pm, 4pm-7pm.

directory

They operate an emergency service - with a small charge - rota available from the tourist office.

physiotherapists
Aufdenblatten t 027 967 4182
Burlet t 079 378 6388

safety on the mountain
avalanche danger - the risk of avalanche is graded from 1 to 5.
1. (green) low, generally risk-free conditions.
2. (yellow) moderate, favourable conditions for the most part.
3. (dark yellow) considerable, partly unfavourable conditions.
4. (orange) high, partly unfavourable conditions.
5. (red) very high, skiing not advised. The risk level is displayed each day at the main lift stations, but if you are in any doubt about where it is safe to ski ask their advice.

food & drink - a skiing holiday is not the time to start a diet. Your body expends energy keeping warm and exercising so it's a good idea to eat a decent breakfast, and carry some chocolate or sweets with you. The body dehydrates more quickly at altitude and whilst exercising. You need to drink lots of water each day to replace the moisture you lose.

rules of conduct - the International Ski Federation publishes conduct rules for all skiers and boarders, as summarised.
1. respect - do not endanger or prejudice the safety of others.
2. control - ski in control, adapting speed and manner to ability, the conditions and the traffic.
3. choice of route - the uphill skier must choose his route so he does not endanger skiers ahead.
4. overtaking - allowed above or below, right or left, but leave enough room for the overtaken skier.
5. entering & starting a run - look up and down the piste when doing so.
6. stopping on the piste - avoid stopping in narrow places or where visibility is restricted.
7. climbing - keep to the side of the piste when climbing up or down.
8. signs & markings - respect these.
9. assistance - every skier must assist at accidents.
10. identification - all involved in an accident (including witnesses) must exchange details.

snow & avalanche forecast
t 187, infoneige t 027 775 2525
i slf.ch

weather
Weather and temperature can change quickly in the mountains. A day that starts off as clear and sunny can end in a whirling blizzard. Even in the resort, air temperature can be very low and the higher you go up the mountain, the colder it gets. A strong wind also lowers the overall temperature considerably.
weather forecast t 162, i meteosuisse.ch

directory

what to wear
Several, thin layers are better than one thick piece. Avoid cotton, which keeps moisture next to the body, so cooling it down. A strong and wind and moisture resistant material such as Goretex is best for outer layers. Gloves and a hat are also essential.

Always wear sunglasses (or goggles when cloudy), preferably wrap-around with shatter-proof lenses giving 100% protection from UVA and UVB rays. No or poor eye protection can cause snowblindness - the eyes water and feel painful and gritty. Treat by resting eyes in a darkened room, and applying cold compresses.

The sun is more intense at high altitude, so re-apply a high factor SPF sun protection (from UVA and UVB rays) regularly, even if overcast and cloudy and particularly after falling or sweating. Don't forget ear lobes, and the underside of the nose.

resort survival

banks & atms
The 3 branches of banks (Credit Suisse, UBS and Raiffeisenbank) are open Mondays-Fridays 9am-12pm, 3pm-6pm. There are also ATMs at the Klein Matterhorn station and below the Beau-Site hotel and a bureau de change at the Bahnhof.

church services
St. Peter's English church (t 027 967 5566) built in 1869, to cater for the number of English visitors. C of E services for are now held every Sunday at 10:30am and 6:30pm - as part of the Intercontinental Church Society so everybody welcome.

internet/email
Alpin Surf (i alpin-surf.ch) has coin operated computers open 9am-12am, CHF 5/10 mins. The Country Bar has 21 terminals while the hotel Post has 2 terminals. The Stoked Internet corner has 7 stations, wifi, 1 hour CHF12, a half hour is CHF7. Most phone boxes also have an internet/email facility.

laundry & dry cleaning
Biner on Steinmatte (t 027 967 2987) and Doli (t 027 967 5100) open Mondays-Fridays and Saturday mornings.

left luggage
You can leave your luggage at the train station 6:30am-9pm for a small charge.

directory

library
Open Mondays, Tuesdays, Thursdays and Fridays 4pm-8pm.

newspapers
English newspapers (and others) - often for the same day - are available from the small kiosk near the Monte Rosa on Bahnhofstrasse and from any of the bookshops. Expect to pay 3 times what you would pay in the UK.

post office
Open Mondays-Fridays 8:30am-12pm, 1:45pm-6pm, Saturdays 8:30am-11am - take a numbered ticket for the queue.

radio
Info Mattertal 97.8 FM broadcasts weather, pistes and snow information in German and English 8:10am-9:10am

shops
Most everything you need is found on Bahnhofstrasse - shops are open daily (except public holidays) 8:30am-12pm, and 2pm-6pm.
supermarkets - Coop, PAM, Primo and Migros. Migros only stocks own-brands and does not sell alcohol. Coop and Migros are open on Sundays and Coop will deliver.
local produce - Josi stocks a good selection of wine and a range of deli food including cheese (open weekdays and Saturdays 9am-12pm, 3pm-7pm and Sundays 4pm-7pm)
clothes - anything from Benetton to Gant, Peak to Mammut, there are numerous clothes shops along or just Bahnhofstrasse.
florists - krönig-perren (t 027 967 2180)
gifts - include Swiss clocks, stuffed St. Bernard dogs and a chocolate memento of that mountain (a Toblerone) in pretty much any size - maybe Orson Welles was right.

ski & snowboard service
An overnight pick-up service (t 027 967 5262), skis are taken away at 6pm and returned for your skiing the next day.

ski lockers/equipment storage
Lockers at the Sunnegga funicular, the Klein Matterhorn and the Gornergrat train station as well as at the Bahnhof. CHF2 for a small locker or ski holder and CHF5 for a big locker. The locker takes your coin as soon as you shut the door, so make sure you have put in/taken out everything you need.

tv channel
The Tele Info Zermatt channel (in bigger shops, cable cars and lift stations) broadcasts a range of information - including ski and weather reports in the morning and again in the early afternoon and local information such as the on-call doctor, local events.

tourist office
Located on Bahnhofstrasse (t 027 966 8100, i zermatt.ch) and open Mondays-Saturdays 8:30am-12pm, 2pm-6pm and Sundays 9:30am-12pm, 2pm-5pm. Most information is available in English.

directory

country survival

customs
UK visitors over 17 can take 200 cigarettes, 50 cigars or 250g of pipe tobacco, 1 litre of spirirts, 2 litres of wine and gifts up to the value of CHF100 out of Switzerland.

electricity
220 volts/50hz ac. Appliances use a 2-pin plug - you can buy adaptors at the airports or in resort.

language
Zermatt is in German-speaking Switzerland, though information is also displayed in French and Italian. English is quite widely spoken.

money
The currency is the Swiss Franc (SFr/CHF) - CHF1 is 100 centimes. Notes come in CHF10, 20, 50, 100, 200, 1,000 and coins in CHF1, 2, 5 and cents 5, 10, 20, 50. In 2004 the average exchange rate for UK£1 was CHF2.2. Some places accept Euros.

passports & visas
UK citizens don't need a visa and can stay for 3 months - your passport should have at least 6 months until expiry. A work permit is needed for a longer stay. All Swiss citizens must carry ID, so it's worth taking your passport with you.

public holidays
December 6 - St Nicholas Day
25 - Christmas Day
26 - St Stephen's day
January 1 - New Year's Day
March 19 - St Joseph's day
March/April Good Friday, Easter Sunday & Monday

telephone
The minimum cost of any call is 60ct and you can pay by phone card (CHF5/10/20, sold at the post office, and train stations), credit card or a Swisscom International Prepaid Card (CHF 10/20/50/100). All local and most international calls are cheaper 5pm-8am. The free international operator is 0800 801 141; international direct enquiries 1159; and national direct enquiries 111. Swisscom, Sunrise and Orange are the mobile phone networks.

time
Switzerland is always 1 hour ahead of the UK.

tipping
Restaurants and hotels are obliged to work a service charge into the bill, so you are don't need to leave an extra tip.

uk embassy & consulates
UK Embassy - Bern t 0313 597 700
Consulate - Geneva t 0227 981 605

water
Tap water is drinkable except where there are signs to the contrary.

glossary

a
arête - a sharp ridge.
avalanche - a rapid slide of snow down a slope.
avalanche transceiver - a device used when skiing off-piste, which can both emit and track a high frequency signal to allow skiers lost in an avalanche or a crevasse to be found.

b
BASI - British Association of Snowsport Instructors.
binding - attaches boot to ski.
black run/piste - difficult, generally steeper than a red piste.
blood wagon - a stretcher on runners used by ski patrollers to carry injured skiers off the mountain.
blue run/piste - easy, generally wide with a gentle slope.
bubble → 'gondola'.
button (or Poma) lift - for 1 person. Skis and boards run along the ground, whilst you sit on a small 'button' shaped seat.

c
cable car - a large box-shaped lift, running on a thick cable over pylons high above the ground, which carry up to 250 people per car.
carving - a recently developed turning technique used by skiers and boarders to make big, sweeping turns across the piste.
carving skis - shorter and fatter than traditional skis, used for carving turns.
chairlift - like a small and uncomfortable sofa, which scoops you and your skis off the ground and carries you up the mountain. Once on, a protective bar with a rest for your skis holds you in place. Can carry 2-6 people.
couloir - a 'corridor' between 2 ridges, normally steep and narrow.
crampons - spiked fittings attached to outdoor or ski boots to climb mountains or walk on ice.

d
draglift or (T-bar) - for 2 people. Skis and boards run on the ground, whilst you lean against a small bar.
drop-off - a sharp increase in gradient.

e
edge - the metal ridge on the border of each side of the ski.

f
FIS - Federation Internationale du Ski.
flat light - lack of contrast caused by shadow or cloud, making it very difficult to judge depth and distance.
freeriding, freeskiing - off-piste skiing.
freestyle - skiing involving jumps.

g
glacier - a slow-moving ice mass formed thousands of years ago and fed each year by fresh snow.
gondola (or bubble) - an enclosed lift, often with seats.

h
heliskiing - off-piste skiing on routes only accessible by helicopter.
high season - weeks when the resort is (generally) at full capacity.

i
itinerary route (yellow) - not groomed, maintained or patrolled.

glossary

Generally more difficult, at least in part, than a black piste. Can be skied without a guide.

k
kicker - jump.

l
lambchop drag ➝ 'rope tow'.
ledgy - off-piste conditions in which there are many short, sharp drop-offs.
low season - beginning and end of the season and the least popular weeks in mid-January.

m
mid season - reasonably popular weeks in which the resort is busy but not full.
mogul - a bump, small or large, on or off piste. A large mogulled area is called a mogul field.

o
off-piste - the area away from marked, prepared and patrolled pistes.

p
parallel turn - skis turn in parallel.
piste - a ski run marked, groomed and patrolled, and graded in terms of difficulty (blue, red or black).
piste basher - a bulldozer designed to groom pistes by smoothing snow.
pisteur - a ski piste patroller.
Poma ➝ 'button lift'.
powder - fresh, unbashed or untracked snow.

r
raquettes ➝ 'snowshoes'.
red run/piste - intermediate, normally steeper than a blue piste, although a flatish piste may be a red because it is narrow, has a steep drop-off or because snow conditions are worse than on other pistes.
rope tow (or lambchop drag) - a constantly moving loop of rope with small handles to grab onto to take you up a slope.

s
schuss - a straight slope down which you can ski very fast.
seasonnaire - an individual who lives (and usually works) in a ski resort for the season.
skis - technology has changed in the last 10 years. New skis are now shorter and wider. When renting, you will be given a pair approx. 5-10cms shorter than your height.
ski patrol - a team of piste patrollers
skins - artificial fur attached to ski base, for ski touring.
snow-chains - chains attached to car tyres so that it can be driven (cautiously) over snow or ice.
snowshoes - footwear resembling tennis rackets which attach to shoes, for walking on soft snow.
spring snow - granular, heavy snow conditions common in late season (when daytime temperatures rise causing snow to thaw and re-freeze).
steeps - a slope with a very steep gradient.

t
T-bar ➝ 'draglift'.

w
white-out - complete lack of visibility caused by enveloping cloud cover.

index

a
accidents 117
accommodation 11, 28
activities
- general 106
- snow 85

air travel 22
airports 19, 22, 115
air zermatt 43, 106, 116
alpin center 42, 49
ambulance 117
aparthotels 39
apartments 40
après-ski 11, 14, 62, 66, 71, 98
ATMs 119
avalanches 45, 118

b
babysitters 108
bad weather 62, 66, 72, 77, 78
banks 119
bars 98
- feature bar 100

bed & breakfast 28
beginners 56
boarders 57, 75
board rental 45
boot rental 44, 45
bus
- around zermatt 25, 27
- to zermatt 24

c
cafés 95
camping 41
car travel 19, 20, 26, 115
car hire 22, 115
casino 107
cervinia 73
chalets 38
chapels 15
childcare 108
children 42, 108
cinema 107, 109
country survival 121
crèche 108
cross-country skiing 85
curling 106
currency 121

d
day-trips 107
DIY holidays 19
doctor 117
driving 19, 20, 115

e
email 111, 119
emergencies 117
equipment rental 44
eurostar 22
eurotunnel 20
events 84
exchange rate 121
experts 56

f
ferries 20
findeln 58, 60
flights 18, 19, 106, 115
food & drink 12, 88

g
garnis 28
geneva 19, 22, 24
glacier express 107
gornergrat 63
guides 49

h
haute route 50, 71, 83
health & safety 117
helicopter 24, 106, 116
heliskiing 85
horse-drawn carriage 26
hostels 37
hotels 28
- feature hotel 32
- budget 36
- luxury 33
- map 31
- mid-range 34

i
ice skating 106
igloos 71
insurance 43, 44, 50, 117
intermediates 56
internet 111, 119
itinerary routes 55, 56, 60, 65, 69, 80

k
kids 42, 108
kindergarten 108
klein matterhorn 67

l
language 15, 111
late night food 97
lessons
- board 46, 48
- booking 47
- children 46
- ski 46, 48

lift passes 42, 108
lifts overview 55
lift stations 11, 25
lift tables
➞ inside back cover
luggage delivery 24
lunchtime 97
luttman/johnson 84

m
maps

index

↳ contents
massages 107
matterhorn, the 10, 14, 54
milan 19, 22, 24
minibus transfer 24
money 121
mountain guides 49
museum 107
music concerts 107

n
nightclubs 105
night-skiing 85
non-skiers 43, 57
nursery 108

o
off-piste 55, 56, 60, 65, 69, 75, 80
off-piste equipment 45
other resorts 25
overland 20

p
package holidays 18
parapenting 106
parking 20, 116
patrouille des glaciers 84
pharmacies 117
pistes overview 54
police 117
post office 120
private rooms 41
public holidays 121
pubs 98

r
rental
 - boards 45
 - boots 45
 - other equipment 45
 - skis 44

reps 18
residences 28, 33
resort survival 119
restaurants 88
 - feature restaurant 90
road travel 19, 20, 26, 115
rothorn 58
rules of conduct 118

s
safety 117
saunas & steam 107
seasonnaires 110
 - before you go 110
 - once you're there 110
self-drive 20
seniors 43
shopping 106, 120
ski areas 12, 55
 ↳ contents
ski club of gb 50, 84
ski maps
 ↳ inside back cover
ski rental 44
ski schools 46
ski touring 82
skiing 12, 55, 58, 63, 67, 73
sledging 85
snowboarders 57, 75
snowfall 13
snowpark, the 57, 69
snowshoeing 85
snowtrain 22
spa 107
sports 106
suggested days 78
summer skiing 43, 57, 69
supermarkets 120

swimming 38, 106

t
take-away food 97
täsch 20
taxis 22, 24, 26
telephones 121
temperatures 13
tipping 121
tobogganing 85
torch-lit descent 85
tour operators 18, 38, 108, 114
tourist office 28, 38, 120
train 19
 - long distance 22
 - local 22, 24, 63
 - swiss pass 22, 43
transfers 18, 19, 22, 115
transport 20
travel
 - around zermatt 25
 - to zermatt 20
triftji bumps 65, 79, 84

u
using the guides 4
using the maps 5

v
valley-floor lift stations 11, 25, 27, 56
volume of people 13

w
walking 26, 43, 57
weather 13
weekends 18, 29, 114
wine 78, 120
work permits 110

z
zum see 71, 78
zurich 19, 22, 24

125

also available…

the snowmole guides to

chamonix mont-blanc
including argentière and full coverage of chamonix's 4 ski areas and the vallée blanche…

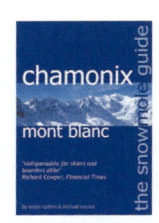

courchevel les 3 vallées
including 1850, 1650, 1550, le praz & la tania and full coverage of the 3 vallées ski area …

la plagne paradiski
including all 10 resorts and full coverage of the paradiski area and the vanoise express ..

les arcs paradiski
including peisey-vallandry & arc 1950 and full coverage of the paradiski area and the vanoise express…

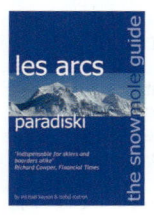

also available…

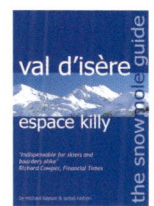

méribel les 3 vallées
including méribel centre, les allues, méribel village & mottaret and full coverage of the 3 vallées ski area…

val d'isère espace killy
including st. foy and full coverage of the espace killy area…

verbier val de bagnes
including full coverage of the 4 vallées from verbier to veysonnaz…

and coming soon the snowmole guides to…

st. anton arlberg
tignes espace killy
ski weekends
alpine secrets

& also the underground network

further information

accuracy & updates
We have tried our best to ensure that all the information included is accurate at the date of publication. However, because places change - improve, get worse, or even close - you may find things different when you get there. Also, everybody's experience is different and you may not agree with our opinion. You can help us, in 2 ways: by letting us know of any changes you notice and by telling us what you think - good or bad - about what we've written. If you have any comments, ideas or suggestions, please write to us at: snowmole, 45 Mysore Road, London, SW11 5RY or send an email to comments@snowmole.com

snowmole.com
Our website is intended as a compliment to our guides. Constantly evolving and frequently updated with news, you will find links to other wintersport related websites, information on our stockists and offers and the latest news about future editions and new titles. We also use our website to let you know of any major changes that occur after we publish the guides. If you would like to receive news and updates about our books by email, please register your details at www.snowmole.com

order

The snowmole guides are available from all major bookshops, wintersports retailers or direct from Qanuk Publishing & Design Ltd. To experience the Alps without leaving home have your next snowmole guide delivered to your door. To order send an email to sales@snowmole.com or fill in the form below and send it to us at Qanuk Publishing & Design Ltd, 45 Mysore Road, London, SW11 5RY.

the snowmole guide to:	ISBN	quantity
chamonix mont blanc	0-9545739-3-5	
courchevel les 3 vallées	0-9545739-5-1	
la plagne paradiski	0-9545739-8-6	
les arcs paradiski	0-9545739-7-8	
méribel les 3 vallées	0-9545739-4-3	
val d'isère espace killy	0-9545739-9-4	
verbier val de bagnes	0-9545739-2-7	
zermatt matterhorn	0-9545739-6-X	

total:
(£6.99 each, postage & packaging free)

I enclose a cheque for £
(made payable to Qanuk Publishing & Design Ltd)

name
address
postcode
tel
email address
(please use block capitals)

Delivery will normally be within 14 working days. The availability and published prices quoted are correct at the time of going to press but are subject to alteration without prior notice. Please note that this service is only available in the UK.

Qanuk would like to keep you updated on new titles in the snowmole range or special offers. If you do not wish to receive such information please tick here ☐
Qanuk has a number of partners in the ski industry, and we may from time to time share your details with those partners if we think it might be of interest to you. If you do not wish us to share your details please tick here ☐

about you

Your comments, opinions and recommendations are very important to us. To help us improve the snowmole guides, please take a few minutes to complete this short questionnaire. Once completed please send it to us at Qanuk Publishing & Design Ltd.

name (Mr/Mrs/Ms) _____
address _____
postcode _____
email address _____
age _____
occupation _____

1. about your ski holiday (circle as appropriate)
how many days do you ski each year?
weekend/1 week/2 weeks/1 month/more
when do you book?
last-minute/1 month before/1-3 months before/3-6 months before/6+ months before
how do you book your holiday?
travel agent/mainstream tour operator/ski-specific tour operator/diy

2. about the snowmole guide
which title did you buy? _____
where and when did you buy it? _____
have you bought any other snowmole guides? _____
if so, which one(s) _____
how would you rate each section out of 5 (1 = useless, 5 = very useful)
getting started _____
the skiing _____
the resort _____
the directory _____
the maps _____
what in particular made you buy this guide? _____
_____
do you have any general comments or suggestions? _____
_____
did you buy any other guides for your holiday? _____
if yes, which one? _____
Qanuk Publishing & Design Ltd may use information about you to provide you with details of other products and services, by telephone, email or in writing. If you do not wish to receive such details please tick here ☐

about us

snowmole / snṓmōl / n. & v. **1** a spy operating within alpine territory (esp. ski resorts) for the purpose of gathering local knowledge. **2** (in full **snowmole guide**) the guidebook containing information so gathered. v. research or compile or process intelligence on an alpine resort or surrounding mountainous area.

the authors
Isobel Rostron and Michael Kayson are snowsport enthusiasts who met while taking time out from real life to indulge their passion - Isobel to get it out of her system and Michael to ingrain it further. Michael's approach having won, they decided that a return to real life was overrated and came up with a cunning plan to make their passion their work. The result was snowmole.

acknowledgments & credits
None of this would have been possible without the help and support of many people:
Patrizia Stähli & Francine Lauber (Zermatt Tourism), Peter & Christine Rostron for their generosity, Will Atkinson for his editorial comments and general suggestions, Andrew Lilley for his invaluable and underpaid proofreading skills, Karin Forster, Anna Worth, Steph Gavin, Adrian Maguire, Robbie Tobias, Anthony Rice, Stephen Elliott, Dan Austin, Zoe Bannister & Jo Tench for their research, Asher Cairns for his assistance and Angela Horne, Julian Horne, Henry & Katie Fyson and Maisie Rostron for their ongoing support.

The publishers would like to thank the following for their kind permission to reproduce their photographs.
front cover: Zermatt Tourism - Toni Mohr
back cover: Office du Tourisme Courchevel 1850 & Office du Tourisme de La Plagne
inside: title page & pages 68 Zermatt Tourism - Zermatt Bergbahnen, pages 10 Zermatt Tourism - Toni Mohr, pages 12 Zermatt Tourism - Mattias Fredriksson, pages 14 & 15 Zermatt Tourism - Kurt Mueller (Matterhorn peak), Toni Mohr (Gornergrat train & mountain chapel) & Valais Tourism (Findeln), pages 59, 64 Zermatt Tourism - Kurt Mueller, page 78 Zermatt Tourism - Oliver Ritz, page 80 Zermatt Tourism - Mattias Fredriksson, pages 79, 81 & 82 Valais Tourism and page 83 Nigel Tench
The remaining photographs are held in the publisher's own photo library and were taken by Isobel Rostron.

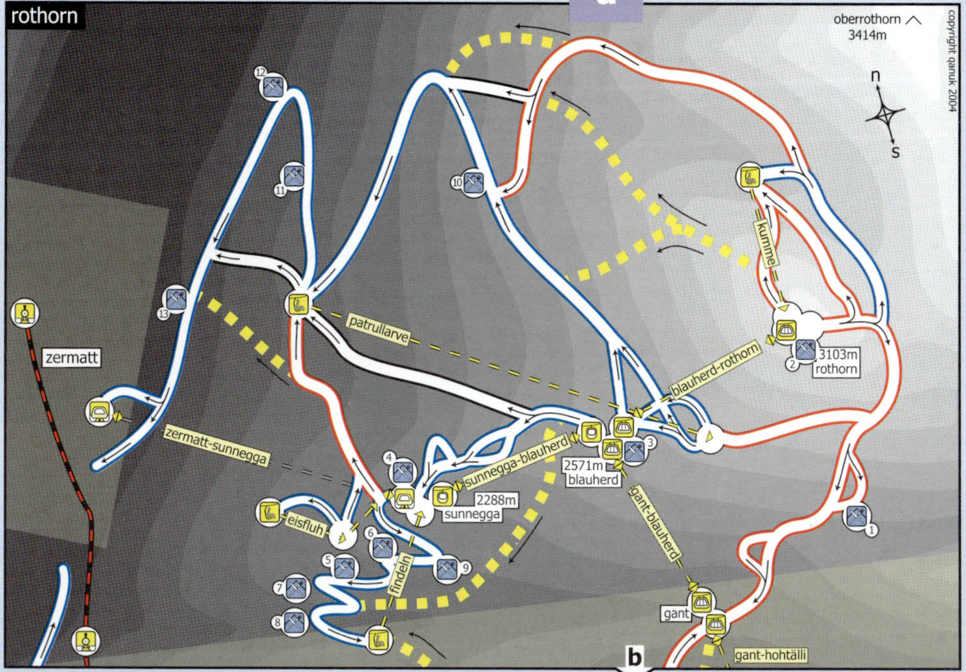

rothorn
a
oberrothorn
3414m
n
s
copyright qanuk 2004
12
11
10
13
zermatt
patrullarve
kumme
3103m
rothorn
2
blauherd-rothorn
zermatt-sunnegga
sunnegga-blauherd
2571m
blauherd
3
4
2288m
sunnegga
eisfluh
6
5
9
findeln
7
8
gant-blauherd
1
gant
gant-hohtälli
b

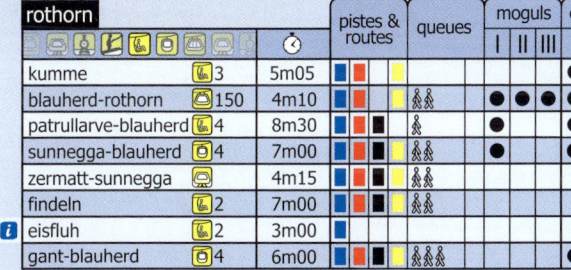

rothorn

		⏱	pistes & routes	queues	moguls	off-piste
kumme	3	5m05	🟦🟥🟨⬛			●
blauherd-rothorn	150	4m10	🟦🟥⬛	≋		●●
patrullarve-blauherd	4	8m30	🟦🟥⬛	≋≋	●	●●
sunnegga-blauherd	4	7m00	🟦🟥⬛	≋≋	●	●
zermatt-sunnegga		4m15	🟦🟥⬛	≋≋		
findeln	2	7m00	🟦	≋	● ●	
i eisfluh	2	3m00	🟦			
gant-blauherd	4	6m00	🟦🟥🟨⬛	≋≋≋		●

i eisfluh — there is a moving carpet from the top of the lift to the sunnegga mid-station

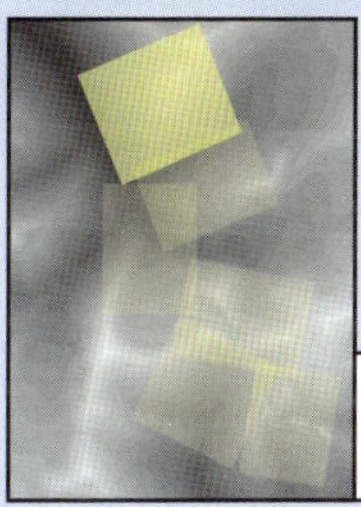

rothorn

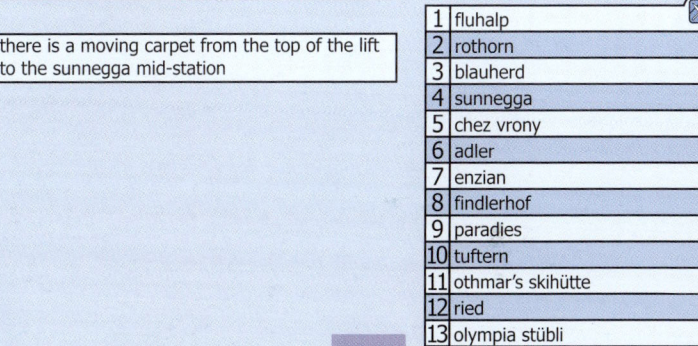

🍴
1	fluhalp
2	rothorn
3	blauherd
4	sunnegga
5	chez vrony
6	adler
7	enzian
8	findlerhof
9	paradies
10	tuftern
11	othmar's skihütte
12	ried
13	olympia stübli

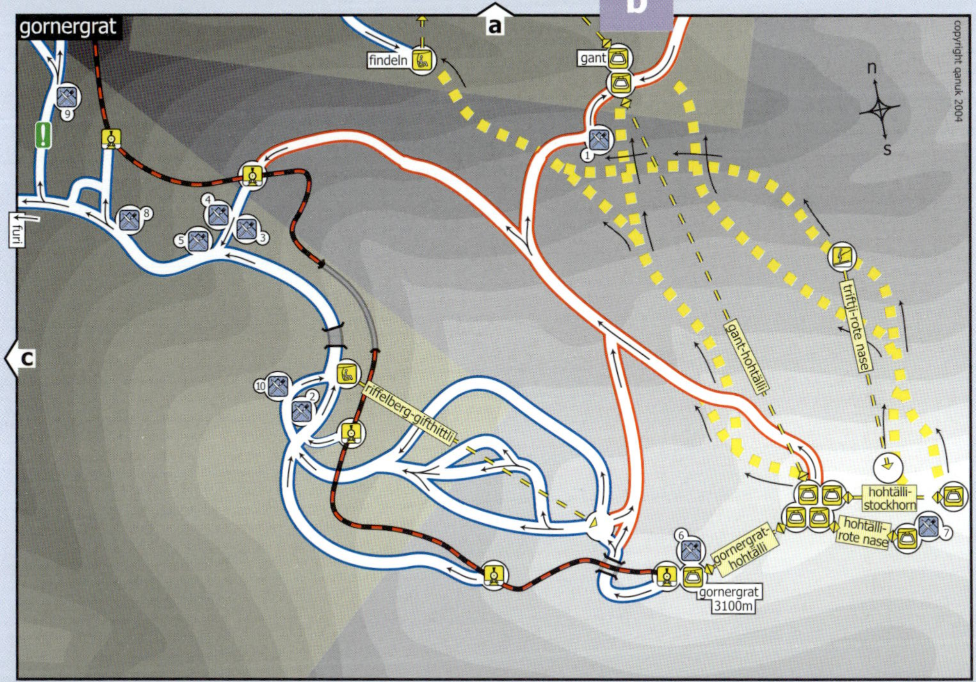
gornergrat
a
findeln
gant
c
furi
n
s
copyright qanuk 2004
1
2
3
4
5
6
7
8
9
10
triftji-rote nase
gant-hohtälli
riffelberg-gifthittli
hohtälli-stockhorn
hohtälli-rote nase
gornergrat-hohtälli
gornergrat 3100m

gornergrat

		⏱	pistes & routes	queues	moguls	off-piste
i	gornergrat-hohtälli	🚡40	5m30	🟥		●● ●●	●●●
	hohtälli-stockhorn	🚡40	5m40	🟥	👥👥	●● ●●	●●●
	hohtälli-rote nase	🚡60	2m30	🟨	👥👥	●● ●●	●●●
i	triftji-rote nase	🚡2	9m15	🟨	👥	●● ●●	●●●
	gant-hohtälli	🚡125	6m25	🟥🟨		●● ●●	●●●
i	riffelberg-gifthittli	🚡6	7m00	🟦	👥👥		●●
i	zermatt-gornergrat	🚞	8m40	🟦			●●

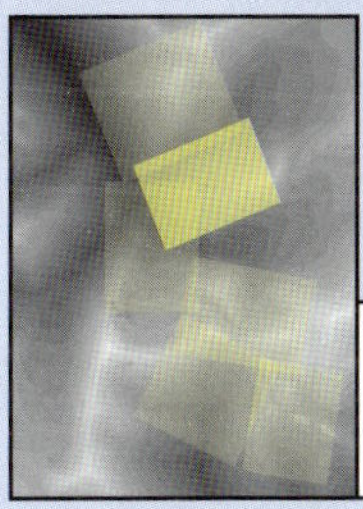

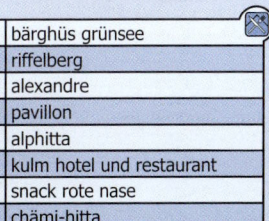

i		
	gornergrat-hohtälli	the entrance to the lift is some way uphill from the gornergrat train station
	triftji-rote nase	very steep - it is best to go in a two to avoid being lifted off the ground
	riffelberg-gifthittli	heated seats!

gornergrat

❌		
1	bärghüs grünsee
2	riffelberg
3	alexandre
4	pavillon
5	alphitta
6	kulm hotel und restaurant
7	snack rote nase
8	chämi-hitta
9	moos
10	riffelberg hotel

b

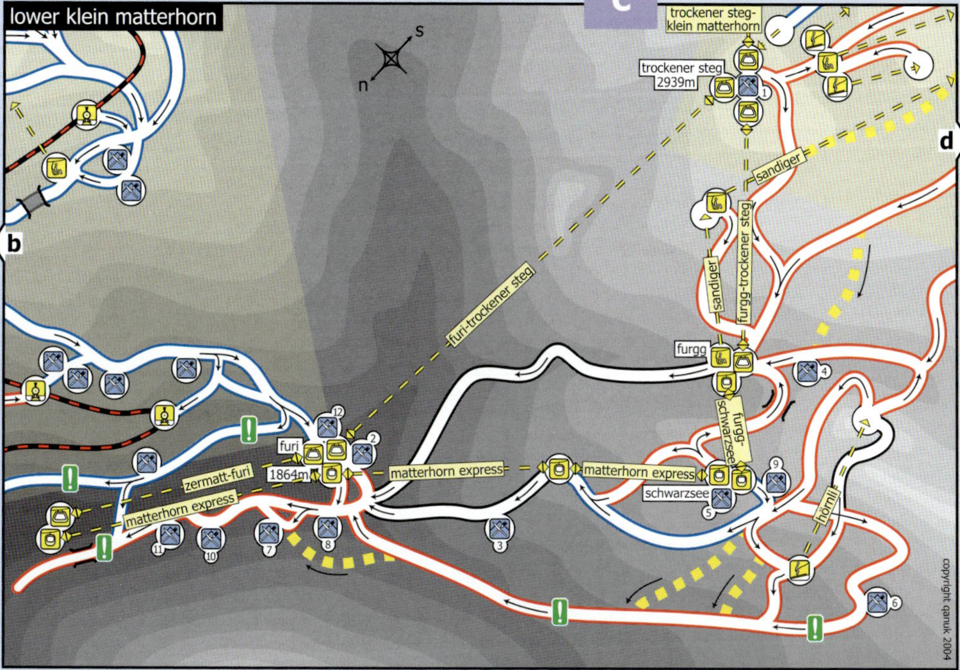
lower klein matterhorn
s
n
b
d
trockener steg-
klein matterhorn
trockener steg
2939m
sandiger
furgg-trockener steg
furi-trockener steg
furgg
furgg-
schwarzsee
matterhorn express
matterhorn express
schwarzsee
hörnli
furi
1864m
zermatt-furi
matterhorn express
1
2
3
4
5
6
7
8
9
10
11
12
copyright qanuk 2004

lower klein matterhorn

		⏱	pistes & routes	queues	moguls I II III	off-piste I II III
	matterhorn express ⬚8	15m45	■■	▨▨		● ●
	zermatt-furi ⬚100	5m40	■■■	▨▨		● ●
	furgg-schwarzsee ⬚4x15	2m20	■■	▨▨	● ● ●	● ●
	hörnli ⬚2	9m50	■		● ●	●
	furi-trockener steg ⬚125	7m35	■■	▨▨	● ●	
	furgg - t'steg ⬚100	6m00	■■	▨▨	● ●	
	sandiger b'den-theo ⬚4	12m00	■■		● ●	●

matterhorn express — has 2 mid-stations, the first at furi and the second at areloid

sandiger b'den-theo — mid-station - don't drag poles under chair as they will get caught

lower klein matterhorn

1. trockener steg
2. furi/simi
3. hermetje
4. käsestube furgg
5. schwarzsee (hotel)
6. stafelalp
7. zum see
8. pizzahütte/farmerhaus
9. iglu-dorf
10. blatten
11. hennustall
12. alm

C

upper klein matterhorn

trockener steg 2939m

klein matterhorn 3885m

trockener steg - klein matterhorn

gandegg

furggsattel

testa 1

testa grigia 3479m

plateau rosa

laghi cime bianche - plateau rosa

bordatini

border

border

CH

I

copyright qanuk 2004

upper klein matterhorn

		pistes & routes	queues	moguls	off-piste
t'steg - klein m'horn	100	8m55	▮▮	▧▧▧▧▧	I II III	I II III
furgg-sattel	6	9m35	▮			
gandegg	2	13m55				
testa 1	2	6m15	▮▮			
plateau rosa	2x2	8m00	▮			

- t'steg - klein m'horn — main link to cervinia; often closed in high winds
- furgg-gletscherbahn — although the top is in italy, you can only ski back down to zermatt
- testa 1 — alternative way to reach italy

upper klein matterhorn

1. trockener steg
2. gandegghütte
3. panorama bar
4. testa grigia

p

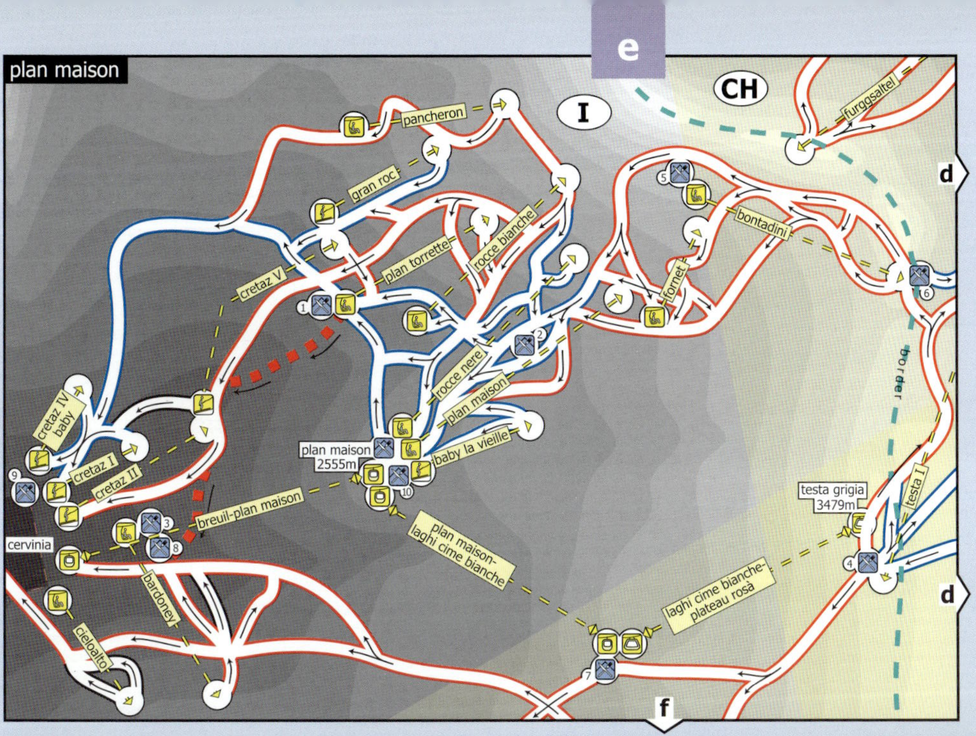

plan maison
e
CH
I
d
d
f
border
furggsaltel
pancheron
gran roc
bontadini
fornet
rocce bianche
plan torrette
cretaz V
rocce nere
plan maison
baby la vieille
plan maison
2555m
cretaz IV
baby
cretaz I
cretaz II
breuil-plan maison
plan maison-
laghi cime bianche
laghi cime bianche-
plateau rosà
testa grigia
3479m
testa I
cervinia
bardoney
cieloalto
1
2
3
4
5
6
7
8
9
10

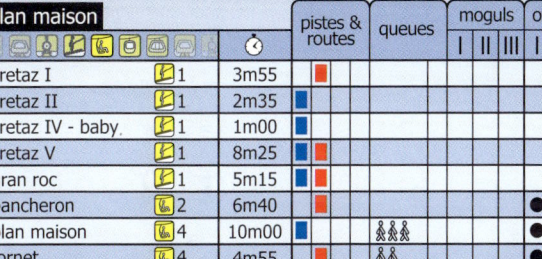

plan maison

		⏱	pistes & routes	queues	moguls off-piste	
	cretaz I	🚡1	3m55	🟥		
	cretaz II	🚡1	2m35	🟥		
ℹ	cretaz IV - baby.	🚡1	1m00	🟦		
	cretaz V	🚡1	8m25	🟦		
	gran roc	🚡1	5m15	🟥		
	pancheron	🚡2	6m40	🟥		
ℹ	plan maison	🚡4	10m00	🟦	〰〰	● ●
	fornet	🚡4	4m55	🟥	〰〰	● ● ●
ℹ	bontadini	🚡4	5m15	🟦	〰〰	● ● ●
	baby la vielle	🚡1	1m00	🟦		
	plan torrette	🚡3	8m30	🟦		
	rocce nere	🚡2	13m15	🟥		● ●
	rocce bianche	🚡2	10m55	🟦		● ●
	l'cime-plateau rosà	🚠140	4m45	🟥	〰〰	
ℹ	cieloalto	🚡2	7m30	🟥		●
	bardoney	🚡2	10m25	⬛ ⬛		● ●
	breuil-plan maison	🚠6	7m55	🟦	〰〰	
	p'maison-laghi-cime	🚠12	11m00	🟥	〰〰	

ℹ	plan maison/fornet/	alternative way to return to zermatt
	bontadini	
	bardoney	often closed

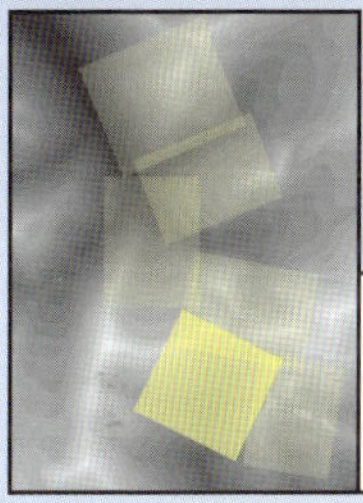

plan maison

1. plan torrette
2. châlet etoile
3. cime bianche
4. testa grigia
5. bontadini
6. rifugio teodulo
7. laghi cime bianche
8. les skieurs d'antan
9. baita cretaz
10. tuktu

e

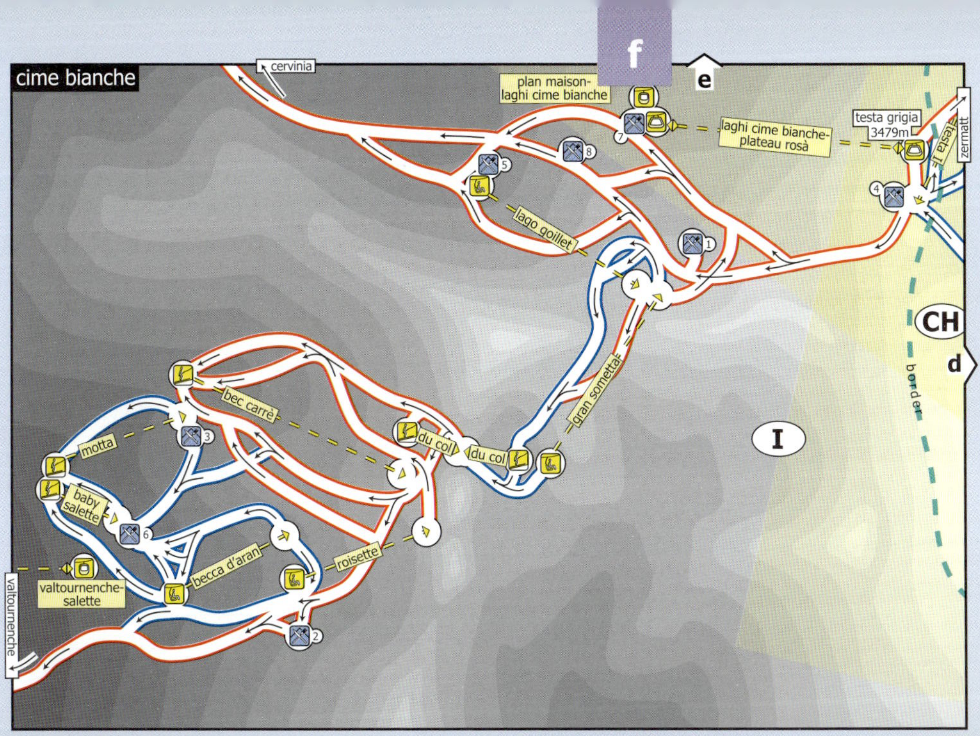
cime bianche
cervinia
plan maison-
laghi cime bianche
f
e
laghi cime bianche-
plateau rosà
testa grigia
3479m
testa I
zermatt
lago goillet
CH
d
border
I
gran sometta
du col
du col
bec carrè
motta
baby
salette
becca d'aran
roisette
valtournenche-
salette
valtournenche
1
2
3
4
5
6
7
8

cime bianche

	⏱	pistes & routes	queues	moguls I II III	off-piste I II III
du col 🎿1	1m00	🟦🟥			
du col 🎿1	1m45	🟦🟥			
grand sometta 🎿1	6m00	🟦🟥			
baby salette 🎿1	1m00	🟦			
becca d'aran 🎿3	6m35	🟥		●	
valtourneche-salette 🎿12	9m20	🟦	≈		
motta 🎿1	5m55	🟦			
bec carrè 🎿1	8m00	🟥		●	
roisette 🎿2	12m35	🟦🟥	≈		
breuil-plan maison 🎿6	7m55	🟦	≈		
p'maison-laghi cime 🎿12	11m00	🟦🟥	≈		
l'cime-plateau rosà 🎿140	4m45	🟦			
lago goillet 🎿3	11m20	🟦🟥			● ●

- p'maison-laghi cime — use to return to zermatt
- du col — appear as 1 lift on the official piste map but there are actually 2 separate lifts

1	bar ventina
2	lo baracon
3	la motta (da felice)
4	testa grigia
5	pousset
6	roisette
7	laghi cime bianche
8	igloo bar

○ ski area key

zermatt (switzerland)
- a - rothorn
- b - gornergrat
- c - lower klein matterhorn
- d - upper klein matterhorn

cervinia (italy)
- e - plan maison
- f - cime bianche

○ the circle indicates the page orientation of the individual ski maps - the arrow points towards the top of the page